通用学术英语教程

主　编　**韩红梅**
副主编　**刘丽红**
编　者　**杨　艳　刘　丽**
　　　　刘向利　刘　杰
　　　　安荣勇　王晓光
　　　　李　英

清华大学出版社
北京

内 容 简 介

本书依据"产出导向法"的教学理论，将"输出驱动"和"输入促成"有机结合，以训练学生掌握各学科中通用的读、写等学术英语技能，开拓其国际视野。本书每个单元包括学术阅读和学术写作两大模块。学术阅读模块每单元围绕一个主题，包括教育、社会、心理、历史、经济和科技等各个方面，辅以多样化练习，由专项基础语言训练过渡到综合性学术能力训练；学术写作模块包括对写作技巧的介绍、结构分析，以及对例文的综合性解析，在此基础上引导学生进行写作输出训练。此外，本书学术阅读部分为"纸质教材+线上补充资源"模式，充分赋能教师的混合式教学实践，促进学生的自主学习。

本书的读者对象：普通高校硕士研究生，致力于提升自身学术能力的三、四年级本科生等。

版权所有，侵权必究。举报：010-62782989，beiqinquan@tup.tsinghua.edu.cn。

图书在版编目（CIP）数据

通用学术英语教程/韩红梅主编.—北京：清华大学出版社，2021.8（2024.7重印）
ISBN 978-7-302-58815-3

Ⅰ.①通… Ⅱ.①韩… Ⅲ.①英语—教材 Ⅳ.①H31

中国版本图书馆CIP数据核字（2021）第157765号

责任编辑：曹诗悦　许玲玉
封面设计：子　一
责任校对：王凤芝
责任印制：刘海龙

出版发行：清华大学出版社
　　　　网　　址：https://www.tup.com.cn, https://www.wqxuetang.com
　　　　地　　址：北京清华大学学研大厦A座　　　邮　　编：100084
　　　　社 总 机：010-83470000　　　　　　　　　邮　　购：010-62786544
　　　　投稿与读者服务：010-62776969, c-service@tup.tsinghua.edu.cn
　　　　质量反馈：010-62772015, zhiliang@tup.tsinghua.edu.cn
印 装 者：三河市天利华印刷装订有限公司
经　　销：全国新华书店
开　　本：185mm×260mm　　　印　　张：11.5　　　字　　数：209千字
版　　次：2021年8月第1版　　　　　　　　　　　印　　次：2024年7月第6次印刷
定　　价：62.00元

产品编号：094101-01

前 言

编写背景

　　学术英语（English for Academic Purposes，EAP）是专门用途英语的一个重要分支，旨在为高校学生用英语进行专业学习提供语言支撑。学术英语作为学生接受国际化高等教育资源和开展学术交流的基本工具，在英语教学体系中日益显现出其重要地位。教育部在 2020 年最新出台的《大学英语教学指南》中强调，学术英语是大学英语教学的有机组成部分。目前，面临经济全球化和教育国际化的时代背景，社会急需专业知识和外语能力兼备的人才。同时，随着大学英语教学改革的深入，研究生层次的英语教学改革也在逐步开展，其中课程设置改革是核心内容。学术英语课程的设置恰逢其时，其目标并不局限于学习英语语言本身，更重要的是使学生借助学术英语的学习，掌握国际学术规范与学术交流技能，培养批判性思维和创新性思维等高层次思维能力，进而成为具备拥有国际视野、能够参与国际事务的国际化人才。

编写目标

　　本教材主要面向普通高校硕士研究生，也适合致力于提升自身学术能力的三、四年级本科生，旨在训练学生掌握各学科中通用的读、写等学术英语交流技能，为自己的专业学习服务。具体着眼于以下几方面的能力培养：

- ❖ 根据单元特定主题搜索和整合信息的能力；
- ❖ 对学术论文结构及主要内容的分析和概括能力，包括文章摘要、研究方法、研究结论等要素；
- ❖ 学术性语言的理解及应用能力；

- ❖ 学术论文的综述及摘要写作能力；
- ❖ 汇报研究成果、参加学术讨论的能力。

教材特色

《通用学术英语教程》的特色主要体现在以下方面：

遵循产出导向法教学理论

教材以产出导向法为依据，根据单元主题和学生认知水平确定恰当的产出目标和产出任务，将"输出驱动"和"输入促成"有机结合，实现学用一体。一方面利用产出任务驱动学习，围绕目标和任务设计产出场景，激发学生学习的动力；另一方面利用输入性学习促进产出，引领学生选择性地学习、掌握学术性语言的特点与表达、学术性文章的篇章结构和写作特点，为完成产出任务做好铺垫。

文章选材凸显学术性特征

与大学本科阶段的通用英语不同，本教材选篇侧重于学术类英语文章，主要以信息性较强的人文科普文章为主，涵盖教育与社会、历史与文化、政治经济和科技创新等方面，用以提升学生的科学和人文素养。同时，所选文章吸收了诸多学者在专业领域的理论和实践研究成果，有利于学生深入理解、归纳、评价和综述各方的观点，培养批判性思维能力，开阔国际化学术视野。

教学重点定位于提升学术素养

与传统的研究生英语读写教材不同，本教材不仅包含阅读专题（包括学术文章阅读、词汇、改写及翻译练习）以夯实学生的语言基础，同时设计了写作专题：既能训练学生搜索和整合文献信息，理解学术性语言的表达特点，分析和概括学术论文结构与关键内容，又能引导学生结合单元主题开展具有一定研究性质的项目活动，如汇报研究成果，撰写文献综述、论文摘要等，全面提升学生的学术素养。

教学与学习资源立体化呈现

为促进学生自主性学习，实现同伴评估、讨论及教师反馈的即时性，本教材打破纸介传播载体的局限，同步配备网络学习平台。平台除承载电子资源外，还具备自主学习检测、同伴在线讨论、实时测验、个人学习记录功能等。此外，该平台还具备教学管理功能，使教师可以更加有效地参与及辅助学生的学习过程。这种立体化的资源体系使得教材可以适用于混合式教学等新型教学模式。

教材内容与结构

本教材共 8 个单元，每单元分为两个模块：学术阅读和学术写作。

学术阅读模块

学术阅读模块每单元围绕一个主题，包括教育、社会、心理、历史、经济和科技等方面。阅读练习的设计层次分明，由专项基础语言训练过渡到综合性学术能力训练。学术阅读模块分为以下几个部分：

- **Topic Exploration**：要求学生在课前上网搜索关于单元主题的背景知识和相关研究，然后通过小组讨论分享所掌握的信息，并以小组汇报的形式展示自己的研究成果。这个练习的主要目的是训练学生运用网络搜索和整合信息、合作与交流，以及口语汇报和展示能力。
- **Reading Comprehension**：包括文章结构分析练习（Text Structure Analysis）、摘要写作练习（Summary Writing）和话题讨论练习（Questions for Discussion）。文章结构分析练习以表格的形式提供文章梗概，让学生根据文章内容填写表格中的缺失信息；摘要写作练习基于结构分析练习中总结的关键信息，让学生运用衔接手段写成一段连贯的、逻辑性强的总结性段落。话题讨论练习是针对文章内容设计的理解性问题，训练学生深入理解和总结文章主要信息，以及口头表达相关信息的能力。
- **Vocabulary**：选择文中的重点词汇和学术词汇设计同义词替换练习和选词填空练习，要求学生能够在口头和书面表达中学会运用该词。
- **Translation**：聚焦阅读中出现和使用频率比较高的句子结构，尤其是固定搭配，以翻译练习的形式呈现，以帮助学生掌握和运用这些结构和搭配。

学术写作模块

学术写作模块的内容首先从分析避免剽窃（Avoiding Plagiarism）的必要性和技巧入手，介绍摘要（Abstract Writing 和 Summary Writing）的写作特点，最后集中介绍了五种学术性论文的结构特点和写作要素：问题解决类文章（Problem-Solution Essay）、原因与影响类文章（Cause and Effect Essay）、比较与对比类文章（Comparison and Contrast Essay）、观点类文章（Opinion Essay）和过程说明类文章（Process Essay）。

每一写作模块主要包括以下几部分内容：导引（Introduction）、特点（Features）、结构（Organization）、例文分析（Sample Writing Analysis）、写作练习（Writing Practice）。由对技巧的简要介绍，过渡到对写作技巧专项特点和结构的分析，以及对例文的综合性解析，在此基础上引导学生进行写作输出训练。

编写团队

《通用学术英语教程》的主编为河北大学韩红梅教授。9 名一线骨干教师共同参与了教材的设计和编写。编写团队本着严谨、务实的态度和创新的理念，经过多年的精心策划和打磨终于完成定稿。参与编写的人员有刘丽红、杨艳、刘丽、刘向利、刘杰、安荣勇、王晓光、李英。在教材编写和修改过程中，有多位专家参与审定和指导。同时，清华大学出版社的曹诗悦编辑及编辑团队也提出了宝贵的修改意见，在此一并表示感谢。

韩红梅

2021 年 6 月

目 录

Unit 1 Academic Integrity 1

Text A   Promoting Academic Integrity in the Online Environment.... 3
Text B   Scientific Fraud 16
Writing Focus   Avoiding Plagiarism... 17

Unit 2 Technology... 27

Text A   Artificial Artists 29
Text B   Information Theory—The Big Data 38
Writing Focus   Summary Writing 39

Unit 3 Economy.. 47

Text A   Making the Most of Trends... 49
Text B   Doctoring Sales.. 59
Writing Focus   Writing an Abstract... 60

Unit 4 Society 67

Text A   Divorce: A Love Story 69
Text B   Growing Grey... 78
Writing Focus   Problem-solution Essay... 79

Unit 5 Education 87

Text A　The Benefits of Being Bilingual 89
Text B　Educating Psyche 99
Writing Focus　Cause and Effect Essay 100

Unit 6 Environmental Protection 109

Text A　The Truth About the Environment 111
Text B　Using Waste, Swedish City Cuts Its Fossil Use 121
Writing Focus　Comparison and Contrast Essay 122

Unit 7 History 131

Text A　The Development of Museums 133
Text B　The Nature and Aims of Archeology 142
Writing Focus　Opinion Essay 143

Unit 8 Psychology 151

Text A　Telepathy 153
Text B　The Psychology of Innovation 163
Writing Focus　Process Essay 164

"清华社英语在线"（TUP English Online）平台使用指南 173

UNIT 1
Academic Integrity

Introduction

Academic dishonesty is a concern at any educational level. Many faculty members feel uncomfortable with delivering courses in the online environment due to a concern that students may find it easier to participate in academic dishonesty than they would in a traditional classroom. The term "scientific fraud" is used to describe intentional misrepresentation of the methods, procedures or results of scientific research, which is unethical and often illegal. As a student, what do you think of academic dishonesty in universities? What if scientific fraud occurs in a researcher's career? In this unit, you'll read two texts which might help you get some information about the two questions.

Learning Objectives

Reading

- Identifying the topic of academic integrity
- Understanding the definition of scientific fraud and some relevant examples
- Summarizing the main ideas using topic-related words or phrases
- Developing the awareness of academic integrity

Writing

- Understanding the definition of plagiarism
- Identifying different ways to avoid plagiarism
- Paraphrasing sentences using proper techniques
- Writing a summary of a text

Unit 1 Academic Integrity

Text A

Topic Exploration

Step 1 Use a library catalogue or Internet sources to search for relevant books or articles about *academic dishonesty*. Share your readings with your group members.

Step 2 Work in groups to prepare a presentation of the books or articles you have previously read. Be sure to include:
- the definition of academic dishonesty
- cases of academic dishonesty in China and abroad
- reasons of academic dishonesty and measures to tackle it

Step 3 Report your work to the whole class.

Reading

Promoting Academic Integrity in the Online Environment[1]

Introduction

1 Academic dishonesty is a concern for many instructors whether

---

1 This text is adapted from *That's My Story and I'm Sticking to It: Promoting Academic Integrity in the Online Environment* by Gibbons, A., Mize, C. D., & Rogers, K. L. (2002, June 24–29). EDEDIA 2002—World Conference on Educational Multimedia, Hypermedia & Telecommunications, Denver, Colorado.

they teach in high school, two-year or four-year institutions. Academic dishonesty may include cheating on examinations, **plagiarizing**, **falsifying** sources or bibliographies, knowingly helping other students cheat, working together on projects that should be completed independently, or **turning in** the same assignment for more than one course (Dean, 2000). With the advent of the Internet and the World Wide Web, there seems to be an attitude among instructors that academic dishonesty is easier because of the availability of material that can easily be **cut and pasted** (Renard, 2000). Course delivery through the online environment may also make it easier for students to cheat since students and instructors do not have the same relationship in an online course as they do in a face-to-face course. Investigating reasons for academic dishonesty in face-to-face and online environments may help **shed** some **light on** ways to develop online coursework that encourages academic **integrity** rather than leaving students to their own devices in which they may be **tempted** toward academic dishonesty.

Reasons for academic dishonesty

2   Measuring the **incidence** of academic dishonesty is usually done through self-report surveys given to students. McCabe and Trevino (1996) reported that from a sample of 1,800 students at nine different state-**sponsored** universities, seventy percent of students surveyed admitted to cheating on exams. Additionally, it was reported that almost fifty percent admitted to working with others on assignments intended to be independent (McCabe & Trevino, 1996).

3   Several factors seem to be associated with the incidence of academic dishonesty. Dean (2000) has identified four of these as patterns seen in the literature: individual characteristics, peer group influences, instructor influences, and institutional policies.

4   Individual characteristics include ideas such as age, gender, social activities and level of academic achievement (Crown & Spiller, 1998; McCabe & Trevino, 1997). Peer group influences indicate that general students' **disapproval** of cheating is most likely to discourage it while peer group acceptance of cheating is likely to encourage it (Crown & Spiller,

1998). Students who take courses with instructors who are perceived as being actively involved and concerned about students are less likely to be involved in academic dishonesty (Crown & Spiller, 1998). Institutional policies that are communicated clearly to students along with the **penalties** for academic dishonesty are likely to reduce the occurrence of academic dishonesty (Crown & Spiller, 1998; McCabe & Trevino, 1996).

5   Considering these factors in regular academic classrooms, it would seem that the same kinds of academic dishonesty would occur in the online environment for the same reasons. Additionally, it may be more tempting or easier to engage in academic dishonesty in an online course than in one that is face to face. Renard (2000) states that although plagiarism is not new, Internet "cheat sites" have made cutting and pasting written sections or even entire papers easier. Students involved in an online course would be using the Internet consistently so the ease of using these sites could be tempting. Additionally, the perception of the instructor being less involved in an online course could encourage academic dishonesty since that is one of the factors that can influence a student's decision to cheat.

Academic dishonesty in the online environment

6   Faculty who design courses to be delivered online may evaluate the time a student should spend in a traditional classroom for an equivalent course, add to it time that should be spent outside of class, and in some cases, add extra requirements due to the student not having to physically drive to a campus-based classroom. Faculty may see these students as being able to connect to the online course and go right to work with the course materials. Often faculty do not consider that the physical environment in which the student is taking the course may not be the **optimal** environment for student success. As students' work begins to be turned in, possibly at a level below the expected standard, the instructor may feel that the **rigor** of the course is being challenged and therefore try to **compensate** by adding additional work. On the other hand, if the work submitted by the student is of a higher than expected standard, the faculty member may suspect that the student may be using inappropriate aids in completing course assignments.

7   In contrast, students may see themselves as being somewhat timid with the technology needed for a particular course. Additionally, these students may not see themselves as having the time to make traditional classroom courses, especially since many online students manipulate their course schedule around work or family obligations (Gibson, 1999). Some students feel that the online courses may be easier than a campus delivery due to a perception about having to only interact with course content, not with the instructor. Students who have done poorly with a particular class may feel that taking the professor **out of the loop** will in some way help them pass the course. In this case, students who may not have the strongest work ethic may be enrolled in courses requiring a stronger work ethic. With all cases, it is easy for the student to become overextended in their time and commitment to the course. This can lead to a situation where students feel that they are required to do too much work for the credit earned in the course.

8   The above mentioned **scenarios** for both faculty and students **set the stage for** many of the factors that can lead to discomfort and the temptation for academic dishonesty. Faculty members who are working to move to the online environment may feel detached from their students, feeling that they really do not have the kind of relationship that they would have if the same students were in a traditional classroom. In a traditional classroom, faculty can "look-in-the-eyes" of their students and make some determination about a student's feelings and needs. Not having this direct contact may lead the faculty member to begin to be suspicious about the rigor of the course and then ultimately the quality and originality of students' assignments.

9   The lack of direct contact and a feeling of detachment also may **profoundly** affect students. Students who already have very busy schedules may be compelled to take online courses due to the belief that they can add their academic work on top of an already busy lifestyle. Once the demands of the course become **overwhelming**, especially in cases where the instructor may feel that the rigor of the course is being challenged, the student may feel that the course requirements are unreasonable for the credit to be awarded. Once students begin to feel that the course requirements are unreasonable, the temptation to use

inappropriate resources to complete course assignments may begin to grow. The temptation can become even stronger when students develop the feeling that they are all alone in their course with little contact or interaction with the instructor or peers.

Designing online courses that promote academic integrity

10   The scenario and concerns mentioned above should not be considered a simple reality of online course delivery. In truth, academic integrity is something that all faculty members must work to promote in any instructional environment. However, with regard to online course delivery, there are design features that can specifically promote academic integrity in this environment.

11   First, online course materials should clearly state that academic dishonesty is not acceptable and then clear examples should be given to illustrate the kind of activities that the student should avoid. Since institutional policies are seen as one factor that has an influence on a student's view of academic dishonesty, it is important to clearly outline for the student what the policy is in all online courses. Further, by giving specific examples, faculty can help students avoid misunderstandings about what the policy actually means. While many students would never turn in someone else's paper as their own, these same students may be tempted to copy and paste sections of their assignments from the Internet, justifying this activity as research.

12   Secondly, online course materials should include a high degree of interaction. Interaction may be developed in several ways and should work to increase the students' contact with the content, the instructor, and peers. A variety of tools can be used to increase interaction such as chat, **bulletin boards**, MOOCs, email, etc. Faculty using these tools can achieve variety in their courses and decrease the perception by students that the instructor is really not there or is not paying attention to the work they are doing. Further, an instructor can use these tools to facilitate cooperative instructional strategies where students work in peer groups. Using cooperative strategies in online courses help to **enculturate** the students into the course by developing a support structure where

students can become knowledgeable of course **norms**. In interactive, well-supported cooperative environments, student peers help to encourage academic integrity and **adherence** to course policies. Faculty who make good use of interaction strategies will reduce the temptation of the student to seek outside help and increase student satisfaction with the course.

13   Lastly, online courses should be designed to include a variety of evaluation methods. With a single evaluation method, a multiple-choice test for example, a true picture of a student's understanding is difficult to achieve. By using multiple evaluation methods, a trend can be identified with regard to student performance and understanding. This is equally true in both online and traditional environments. In a traditional classroom where a student may be very quiet during the semester and three multiple choice exams and a final examination are used for the course grade, it can be difficult to determine if the student understands the material, simply is good at memorization, or cheats. In courses that use multiple evaluation methods, the trend for a student's work can be compared to individual assignments. If a situation occurs where one paper is turned in at a higher level of understanding or quality than has been seen in other course interactions, the possibility of academic dishonesty may be present. Likewise, a student's work trend can be used to guide the student to higher levels of understanding. As students come to realize that their work is being viewed and evaluated, and that feedback is being given, they will feel more attached to the course environment, and academic integrity will be promoted.

Final thoughts

14   There are no easy answers to the many questions that are associated with online course delivery. It is important to understand that many different people who become involved in online learning do so for many different reasons. By understanding these reasons, courses can be designed in a manner that can facilitate a faculty member's satisfaction as well as the success of students. Through the process students will have greater opportunity to grow, be successful, and have a high degree of academic integrity.

References

Crown, D. F., & Spiller, M. S. (1998). Learning from the literature on collegiate cheating: A review of empirical research. *Journal of Business Ethics*, *17* (6), 683–700.

Dean, G. R. (2000). Academic dishonesty and the community college. *ERIC Digest*: EDO-JC-00-7.

Gibson, C. C. (1999). *Distance learners in higher education: Institutional responses for quality outcomes*. Madison, Wisconsin: Atwood Publishing.

McCabe, D. L., & Trevino, L. K. (1996). What we know about cheating in college: Longitudinal trends and recent developments. *Change*, *28* (1), 28–33.

McCabe, D. L., & Trevino, L. K. (1997). Individual and contextual influences on academic dishonesty: A multi-campus investigation. *Research in Higher Education*, *39* (3), 379–396.

Moore, M. G., & Kearsley, G. G. (1996). *Distance education: A system view*. Belmont, California: Wadsworth Publishing.

Renard, L. (2000). Cut and paste 101: Plagiarism and the Net. *Educational Leadership*, *57* (4), 38–42.

Words and Phrases

adherence /ədˈhɪərəns/ *n.* when someone behaves according to a particular rule, belief, principle, etc. 坚持；依附；忠诚
e.g. The deployed services must be monitored and managed for quality of service and adherence to non-functional requirements.

bulletin board /ˈbʊlətɪn-bɔːd/ *n.* board on the wall that you put information or pictures on 布告栏
e.g. Our teacher put our pictures up on the bulletin board.

compensate /ˈkɒmpənseɪt/ *v.* to replace or balance the effect of something bad 抵消；补偿
e.g. The official's promise to compensate people for the price rise clearly hadn't been worked out properly.

cut and paste piece together by excerpting and combining

			fragments from multiple sources 剪贴
		e.g.	This manuscript was cut and pasted from the author's doctoral dissertation.
disapproval	/ˌdɪsəˈpruːvəl/	n.	an attitude that shows you think that someone or their behavior, ideas, etc. are bad or not suitable 不赞成，反对
		e.g.	His action had been greeted with almost universal disapproval.
enculturate	/ɪnˈkʌltʃəˌreɪt/	v.	to get into the process by which an individual learns the traditional content of a culture and assimilates its practices and values 使适应某种文化
		e.g.	They want to solve the transgenerational problem to enculturate people into this society.
falsify	/ˈfɔːlsɪfaɪ/	v.	to change figures, records, etc. so that they contain false information 篡改，伪造
		e.g.	The file was altered to falsify the evidence.
incidence	/ˈɪnsɪdəns/	n.	the number of times something happens, especially crime, disease, etc. 发生率
		e.g.	The incidence of this disease has dropped considerably in the past few years.
integrity	/ɪnˈtegrəti/	n.	the quality of being honest and strong about what you believe to be right 正直，诚实
		e.g.	They said the greatest virtues in a politician were integrity, correctness and honesty.
norm	/nɔːm/	n.	a required or agreed standard amount, etc. 规范；标准
		e.g.	Deviation from the norm is not tolerated.
optimal	/ˈɒptəməl/	adj.	the best or most suitable 最佳的，最优的
		e.g.	The network bandwidth optimal allocation mechanism in new generation network is investigated in this paper.
out of the loop			to be or not be part of a group of people who make important decisions 在局外，出圈
		e.g.	These activists don't want to feel out of the loop.
overwhelming	/ˌəʊvəˈwelmɪŋ/	adj.	very large or greater, more important, etc. than any other 巨大的，极大的
		e.g.	The task won't feel so overwhelming if you break it down into small, easy-to-accomplish steps.
penalty	/ˈpenlti/	n.	a punishment for breaking a law, rule or contract

			刑罚；惩罚
		e.g.	The maximum penalty is up to 7 years imprisonment or an unlimited fine.
plagiarize	/ˈpleɪdʒəˌraɪz/	*v.*	to take words or ideas from another person's work and use them in your work, without stating that they are not your own 剽窃，抄袭
		e.g.	On no account are students allowed to plagiarize in essay writing.
profoundly	/prəˈfaʊndli/	*adv.*	extremely 深刻地
		e.g.	We are all profoundly grateful for your help and encouragement.
rigor	/ˈrɪɡə/	*n.*	great care and thoroughness in making sure that something is correct 严密；严格
		e.g.	This crime must be treated with the full rigor of the law.
scenario	/səˈnɑːriəʊ/	*n.*	a situation that could possibly happen 场景；方案
		e.g.	In the worst case scenario, you could become a homeless person.
set the stage for			to prepare for something or make something possible 为……做好准备
		e.g.	More importantly, it set the stage for the long process of economic reform and modernization.
shed light on			to provide new information that makes a difficult subject or problem easier to understand 为……提供线索；使……清楚地显出
		e.g.	A new approach offers an answer, and may shed light on an even bigger question.
sponsor	/ˈspɒnsə/	*v.*	to give money to a sports event, theater, institution, etc., especially in exchange for the right to advertise 赞助；支持
		e.g.	The bank had offered to sponsor him at university.
tempt	/tempt/	*v.*	to try to persuade someone to do something by making it seem attractive 吸引；引诱；怂恿
		e.g.	The offer of free credit tempted her into buying a new car.
turn in			to give a piece of work you have done to a teacher, your employer, etc. 上交；归还
		e.g.	Have you all turned in your homework assignments?

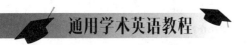

Reading Comprehension

Task 1 Text A can be divided into the following five sections. Read the text carefully and work in pairs to find the main idea of each section. Then complete the following table.

Section	Main Idea
Introduction (Para. 1)	• Academic dishonesty is a _____ for many instructors whether they teach in high school, two-year or four-year institutions, which may include cheating on _____, _____, _____, or _____, knowingly helping _____, working together on _____, or turning in _____. • Reasons for academic dishonesty to be easier than before: 1) _____ 2) _____
Reasons for academic dishonesty (Paras. 2–5)	• Four factors seem to be associated with the incidence of academic dishonesty: 1) _____ 2) _____ 3) _____ 4) _____
Academic dishonesty in the online environment (Paras. 6–9)	Two scenarios for both faculty and students set the stage for factors that can lead to academic dishonesty. • For faculty: 1) Faculty who design online courses may _____ a student should spend in a traditional classroom for an equivalent course, and _____ which make it harder for the students to get the credit. 2) Not having direct contact may lead the faculty member to begin to _____ and then ultimately _____. • For students: 1) Once the demands of the course become _____, especially in cases where the instructor may feel that _____, students may feel that _____, the temptation to use inappropriate resources to complete course assignments may begin to grow. 2) The temptation can become even stronger when students develop the feeling that _____.

Designing online courses that promote academic integrity (Paras. 10–13)	• In order to promote academic integrity, online course materials should: 1) _____ 2) _____ 3) _____
Final thoughts (Para. 14)	• Many different people who become involved in online learning do so for many different reasons, by which courses can be designed in a manner that can facilitate _____ as well as the _____.

Task 2 Based on the information in Task 1, write a summary of the text in 80–100 words. Try to make your paragraph logical and coherent.

Task 3 Work in groups to discuss the following questions.

1. What kind of method did McCabe and Trevino choose to measure the incidence of academic dishonesty? What was the result?
2. In online course environment, what will the faculty member suspect if the work submitted by a student is of a higher than expected standard?
3. In order to promote academic integrity, which tools can be used to increase the students' interaction?
4. What are the effects of students' cheating in academic studies?
5. What do people tend to do in face of increasing academic dishonesty?

Vocabulary

Task 1 For each sentence there are four choices marked A, B, C, and D. Choose the one that best keeps the meaning with the underlined part.

1. What made Reagan extraordinary, beyond his communicative skills, was his resolute <u>adherence</u> to core beliefs.

   A. attachment   B. insistence   C. adoption   D. patience

2. That must <u>tempt</u> them to say yes to ideas of dubious originality.

   A. increase　　　B. promote　　　C. entice　　　D. prevent

3. Excessive conformity is usually caused by fear of <u>disapproval</u>.

   A. objection　　　B. disappointment　　　C. demand　　　D. influence

4. It is designed only to maintain minimum standards, not to assure an <u>optimal</u> decision.

   A. rational　　　B. responsible　　　C. opposite　　　D. ideal

5. The hospital staff were very apologetic but that couldn't really <u>compensate</u>.

   A. resist　　　B. atone　　　C. rebate　　　D. revive

6. Using cooperative strategies in online courses helps to <u>enculturate</u> the students into the course by developing a support structure where students can become knowledgeable of course norms.

   A. acculturate　　　B. encourage　　　C. enable　　　D. encounter

7. The tone of his book is <u>consistently</u> negative, occasionally arrogant, and often superficial.

   A. remarkably　　　B. particularly　　　C. always　　　D. especially

8. The corporation is <u>sponsoring</u> several athletes and teams here in the U.S.

   A. supporting　　　B. dismissing　　　C. encouraging　　　D. inspiring

9. She was praised for her fairness and high <u>integrity</u>.

   A. honesty　　　B. intelligence　　　C. personality　　　D. responsibility

10. Obviously, the court had been <u>profoundly</u> influenced by the progressive upheaval.

    A. extremely　　　B. exactly　　　C. probably　　　D. deeply

Unit 1　Academic Integrity

Task 2　*Complete the following sentences with the words and phrases given below. Change the form if necessary.*

plagiarism	falsify	shed light on	penalty
overwhelming	incidence	norm	turn in
rigor	scenario		

1. Theories that have been _____ must be ruthlessly rejected.

2. However, the new rule does not list any _____ provisions for violators, which arouses doubts over how the new legislation will be implemented.

3. Consider the _____ where a website allows you to use the functions of a partner website, but the partner site is not allowed to know who you are.

4. The proposal has been given _____ support.

5. I explained that the students were refusing to _____ assignments, whether they were as simple as a crossword puzzle or as difficult as an essay.

6. Obviously journalists should not fabricate the news, nor should they _____—that is, copy without attribution—another person's work.

7. A new approach offers an answer, and may _____ an even bigger question.

8. As CEO, Ballmer brought a new level of business _____ to Microsoft.

9. Poverty is one of the reasons for the high _____ of crime in this district.

10. Is procrastination the _____ or does your company drive productivity and results?

Translation

Task 1　*Translate the following paragraph into Chinese.*

　　The scenario and concerns mentioned above should not be considered a simple reality of online course delivery. In truth, academic integrity is something that all faculty members must work to promote in any instructional environment. However, with regard to online course delivery, there are design features that can specifically promote academic integrity in this environment.

___

___

___

Task 2   Translate the following paragraph into English with the help of the words in brackets.

随着每年研究生招生人数的不断上升，毕业论文成为头等大事。很多学生写不出论文，想走捷径，于是选择剽窃论文。他们将一篇或几篇论文内容直接剪贴到自己的论文里而不做任何修改，这使得论文剽窃率逐年上升。作为研究人员，我们在写论文时应该坚持学术诚信，为个人的学术研究做好准备。（plagiarize, cut and paste, incidence, adherence, set the stage for）

___

___

___

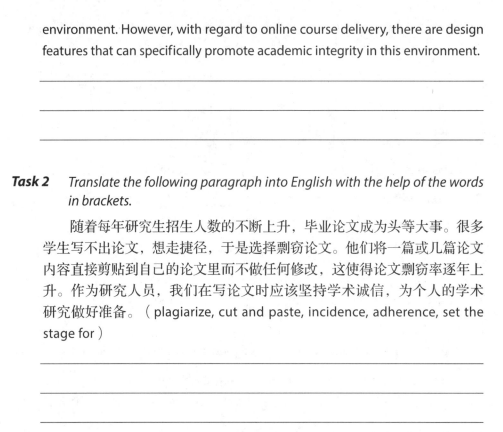

Text B Scientific Fraud

Read **Text B** and do the online exercises.

Unit 1 Academic Integrity

Avoiding Plagiarism

Introduction

Basically, plagiarism means taking ideas or words from a source (e.g. a book or a journal) without giving credit (acknowledgement) to the author. It is seen as a kind of theft, and considered to be an academic crime. In academic work, ideas and words are seen as private property belonging to the person who first thought or wrote them. Therefore, it is important for all students to understand the meaning of plagiarism and learn how to prevent plagiarism in their work.

Exercise 1 Discuss the following questions.

1. Have you heard of any cases of plagiarism recently? Why do you think students plagiarize in academic writing? Share your ideas within your group.

   _____

   _____

2. Work with a partner, add to the list of the reasons why students must avoid plagiarism.
   - To show that they understand the rules of the academic community;
   - To help them develop their own thinking;
   - _____
   - _____
   - _____

Types of Plagiarism

Although plagiarism essentially means copying somebody else's work, it is not always easy to define. In general, anything that is not common knowledge or your own ideas and research (published or not) must be cited or referenced. In academic writing, there are multiple types of plagiarism.

- Direct copying

This is the most obvious type of plagiarism. It's using another person's work completely unaltered and without referencing the source.

- Improper paraphrasing

Improper paraphrasing is considered a common form of plagiarism. This occurs when one copies phrases from another work and changes just a few words without attributing these ideas to the original author. Learning how to properly paraphrase is a vital component of good writing. To correctly paraphrase, you need to use your own words and cite the source of the original work.

- Self-plagiarism

It might not seem wrong to reuse works that you've written in the past—but it actually is. The problem is that this work has already been evaluated. So, unless you acknowledge that you're using your own previous findings, it will be classified as plagiarism.

- Piling up sources

Usually, this one is more of an unintentional case of plagiarism. The main characteristic of it is that the work only contains source materials. They may be properly cited, but if there's no original thoughts or ideas from the author of the paper—it's still plagiarism.

Exercise 2 Tick the following situations in which plagiarism occurs, and state the reasons.

_____ Copying a paragraph, but changing a few words and giving a citation.

_____ Cutting and pasting a short article from a website, with no citation.

_____ Taking a quotation from a source, giving a citation but not using quotation marks.

_____ Using a paragraph from an essay you wrote and had been marked the previous semester, without citation.

_____ Using the results of your own research (e.g. from a survey you did), without citation.

_____ Taking a graph from a textbook, giving the source.

_____ Giving a citation for some information but misspelling the author's name.

Ways to Avoid Plagiarism

In academic research, you need to use outside sources either from a library or from the Internet. If you cannot cite sources properly, it's easy to fall into the trap of plagiarism. There are three ways to avoid plagiarism in academic writing: quoting, paraphrasing, and summarizing. Quoting passages allows you to include the specific words and phrases in the original text of other authors, while paraphrasing and summarizing allows you to interpret a text by using your own words. Either way, referring to outside sources makes your own ideas and your essay more credible.

Quoting	• Reference the original source by inserting the author, year of publication and/or page number of the original source. • The text produced is the exact length of the original text quoted. • Use the original author's exact words, and put quotation marks around quoted texts.
Paraphrasing	• Reference the original source. • The text produced may be shorter or longer than the original text. • Use your own words.
Summarizing	• Reference the original source. • The text is much shorter than the original text. • Must use your own words, usually with a very limited use of quotations.

1. **Quoting**

Quoting, or direct quotation, means bringing the original words of a writer into your work. Quoting is effective in some situations, but should not be overused. They can be valuable:

- when the original words express an idea in a distinctive way;
- when the original is more concise than your summary could be;
- when the original version is well-known.

Note that quotation marks are used around the words which must be quoted exactly as they are in the original. For example:

Dombrowski (2013) states that emotional intelligence is "our ability to understand our own emotions and the emotions of others".

Lightbrown and Spada (2003) claims that the first language acquisition is remarkable for "the high degree of similarity which we see in the early language of education".

Short quotations are placed within quotation marks and are cited using an in-text citation with the expected formatting style (APA, MLA, etc.). If you are quoting passages that are longer than 40 words, you should indent the quoted text. In this case, quotation marks are not needed.

2. **Paraphrasing**

Quotations should not be overused, so you must learn to summarize and paraphrase in order to include other writers' ideas in your work. Paraphrasing and summarizing are normally used together in essay writing to avoid the risk of plagiarism. Summarizing aims to **reduce** the original information to a suitable length, while paraphrasing attempts to **restate** the relevant information by changing the words or structure of the original text.

Paraphrasing involves writing a text so that the language is significantly different while the content stays the same. An effective paraphrase usually:

- has a different structure to the original;
- has mainly different vocabulary;
- retains the same meaning;
- keeps some phrases from the original that are in common use.

<u>Techniques for Paraphrasing</u>:

Here are some techniques you may use when paraphrasing. You need to change the words, word forms and grammatical structure as much as possible, to ensure that a sequence of three words will not be the same as the original. Remember that in practice, the following techniques can be used at the same time.

(a) Changing vocabulary by using synonyms

Synonyms are words or phrases that mean the same thing. Here are some examples using synonyms:

The Scientists' experiment <u>produced</u> an unexpected <u>result</u>.
The Scientists' experiment <u>generated</u> an unexpected <u>outcome</u>.

Despite this, many central city areas <u>have lost their population</u>.
Despite this, many central city areas <u>experienced a decrease in population</u>.

The study <u>shows</u> the <u>need</u> of taking a much broader view in the matter.
The study <u>demonstrates</u> the <u>necessity</u> of taking a much broader view in the matter.

(b) Changing word class

You may also change the word class when paraphrasing. Here are some examples:

This problem can't be <u>solved</u> unless we <u>control</u> atomic energy <u>internationally</u> and <u>eliminate</u> war.
There is no <u>solution</u> to this problem except the <u>international control</u> of atomic energy and the <u>elimination</u> of war.

Some athletes <u>use</u> drugs <u>illegally</u> to make their bodies <u>stronger</u>.
Some athletes enhance their body <u>strength</u> through the <u>illegal use</u> of drugs.

He <u>ends</u> his speech by <u>sharply criticizing</u> the economic situation.
The <u>conclusion</u> of his speech contained some <u>sharp criticism</u> of the economic situation.

(c) Changing sentence structure

When you paraphrase you can't simply replace a few words of the original; that's known as patchwriting and it's a form of plagiarism. To properly paraphrase, you must also change the sentence structure. For example, if the sentence was originally in the active voice, change it to passive voice. Here are some examples of paraphrasing sentences:

Every year, thousands of tourists visit Niagara Falls.
Niagara Falls is visited by thousands of people every year.

An increasing number of people are buying what they need online.
The number of people who buy what they need online is on the increase.

Doctors should be responsible for educating their patients about how to improve their health.
Educating patients about improving their health should be the responsibility of doctors.

Exercise 3 What are the differences between paraphrasing and summarizing?

_____

_____

3. Summarizing

Summarizing means reducing the length of a text but keeping the major points. It is a shortened version of an essay. In your summary, you state the main idea in your own words, but specific examples and details are left out.

Here are the stages you may follow when summarizing an essay:
- Read the original text carefully and check any new or difficult words;
- Underline or highlight the key points;
- Make notes of the key points, paraphrasing where possible;
- Write the summary from your notes, organizing the structure if needed;
- Check the summary to ensure it is accurate and nothing important has been changed or lost.

Sample Essay Analysis

Railway Manias

In 1830 there are a few dozen miles of railways in all the world—chiefly consisting of the line from Liverpool to Manchester. By 1840, there were over 4,500 miles, by 1850 over 23,500. Most of them were projected in a few bursts of speculative frenzy known as the "Railway Manias" of 1835–1837 and especially in 1844–1847; most of them were built in large part with British capital, British iron, machines and know-how. These investment booms appear irrational, because in fact few railways were much more profitable to the investor than other forms of enterprise, most yielded quite modest profits and many none at all: in 1855 the average interest on capital sunk in the British railways was a mere 3.7 percent.

(From *The Age of Revolution* by Eric Hobsbawm, 1995, p. 45)

Exercise 4 Read the essay above and then compare the following five paragraphs which use ideas and information from the essay. Decide which paragraphs are plagiarized and which are acceptable, and give your reasons.

(a) Between 1830 and 1850 there was very rapid development in railway construction worldwide. Two periods of especially feverish growth were 1835–1837 and 1844–1847. It is hard to understand the reason for this intense activity, since railways were not particularly profitable investments and some produced no return at all (Hobsbawm, 1995: 45).

(b) There were only a few dozen miles of railways in 1830, including the Liverpool to Manchester line. But by 1840 there were over 4,500 miles and over 23,500 by 1850. Most of them were built in large part with British capital, British iron, machines and know-how, and most of them were projected in a few bursts of speculative frenzy known as the "railway manias" of 1835–1837 and especially in 1844–1847. Because most yielded quite modest profits and many none at all these investment booms appear irrational. In fact few railways were much more profitable to the investor than other forms of enterprise (Hobsbawm, 1995: 45).

(c) As Hobsbawm (1995) argues, nineteenth century railway mania was partly irrational: "because in fact few railways were much more profitable to the investor than other forms of enterprise, most yielded quote modest profits and many none at all: in 1855 the average interest on capital sunk in the British railways was a mere 3.7 percent." (Hobsbawm, 1995: 45).

(d) Globally, railway networks increased dramatically from 1830 to 1850; the majority in short periods of "Mania" (1835–1837 and 1844–1847). British technology and capital were responsible for much of this growth, yet the returns on the investment were hardly any better than comparable business opportunities (Hobsbawm, 1895: 45).

(e) The dramatic growth of railways between 1830 and 1850 was largely achieved using British technology. However, it has been claimed that much of this development was irrational because few railways were much more profitable to the investor than other forms of enterprise; most yielded quite modest profits and many none at all.

Writing Practice

Task 1 *Read the following paragraph from an article titled "The Mobile Revolution", published in the journal* Development Quarterly *(Issue 34, pages 85–97, 2012) by K. Hoffman. Introduce a quotation of the main point of the paragraph, referring to its source.*

In such countries the effect of phone ownership on GDP growth is much stronger than in the developed world, because the ability to make calls is being offered for the first time, rather than as an alternative to existing landlines. As a result, mobile phone operators have emerged in Africa, India and other parts of Asia that are larger and more flexible than Western companies, and which have grown by catering for poorer customers, being therefore well-placed to expand down market. In addition, Chinese phone makers have successfully challenged the established Western companies in terms of quality as well as innovation. A further trend is the provision of services via the mobile network which offers access to information about topics such as healthcare and agriculture.

Task 2 *Use the techniques that you have learned to paraphrase the following text.*

More than three million shipwrecks are believed to lie on the sea bed, the result of storms and accidents during thousands of years of sea-borne trading. These wrecks offer marine archeologists valuable information about the culture, technology, and trade patterns of ancient civilizations, but the vast majority have been too deep to research. Scuba divers can only operate down to 50 meters, which limits operations to wrecks near the coast, which have often been damaged by storms or plant growth. A few deep sea sites (such as Titanic) have been explored by manned submarines, but this kind of equipment has been too expensive for less famous subjects. However, this situation has been changed by the introduction of a new kind of mini submarine: the automatic underwater vehicle (AUV). This cheap, small craft is free moving and does not need an expensive mother-ship to control it. Now a team of American archeologists are planning to use an AUV to explore an area of sea north of Egypt, which was the approach to a major trading port 4,000 years ago.

Task 3 *Read the following text and write a summary of it in a maximum of three sentences.*

In recent years, emotions have become the subject of study for scientists researching the brain and how we learn. Our ability to understand our own emotions and the emotions of others has been given the name "emotional intelligence". In his book *Frames of Mind* (1984), Howard Gardner put forward a theory of seven intelligences: linguistic intelligence, logical-mathematical intelligence, spatial intelligence, musical intelligence, bodily-kinesthetic intelligence, interpersonal intelligence, and intrapersonal intelligence. These last two kinds of intelligences are related. Interpersonal intelligence means understanding other people and being able to cooperate with others. All sorts of successful people from teachers to religious leaders and politicians probably display these skills to a high degree. Intrapersonal intelligence involves the same abilities applied to ourselves, in other words, being sensitive to our own feelings and being aware of our own strengths and weaknesses. Although Gardner himself did not use the term "emotional intelligence", it is now widely used to refer to interpersonal and intrapersonal intelligences.

Source: Dombrowski, E., Rotenberg, L., & Bick, M. (2007). *Theory of Knowledge: Course Companion*. Oxford: Oxford University Press.

UNIT 2
Technology

Introduction

With the rapid development of information technology, software has been built to create artworks. As a result, much of the new work of this period demonstrated a clear "computer aesthetic", thus eliciting divergent views about computer-produced art.

Information theory has promoted the development of all sorts of communication—from DVD players and the genetic code of DNA to the physics of the universe. It enables data to be sent electronically and has therefore had a major impact on our lives. What are people's attitudes towards computer-produced art? How can information theory be applied to human communication? In this unit, you'll read two texts which might help you get information about these questions.

Learning Objectives

Reading

- Understanding people's different responses to computerized art
- Learning about the application of information theory
- Summarizing the main ideas using topic-related words or phrases
- Developing ideas about computer-produced art and information theory

Writing

- Understanding the features of summary writing
- Identifying steps to write a summary
- Analyzing the use of transitional signals in a summary
- Writing a summary

Unit 2　Technology

Text A

Topic Exploration

Step 1　Use a library catalogue or Internet sources to search for a piece of music or a painting created by computers. Share the music/painting with your group members.

Step 2　Work in groups to discuss the following questions.
- What are the differences between computer-produced and human-produced music/paintings?
- Which one do you prefer, computer-produced art or human-produced art?

Step 3　Report your discussion results to the whole class.

Reading

Artificial Artists[1]

1　　The Painting Fool is one of a growing number of computer programs which, so their makers claim, possess creative talents. Classical music by an artificial composer has had audiences **enraptured**, and even **tricked** them into believing a human was behind the score. Artworks painted by a robot have sold for thousands of dollars and been hung in **prestigious**

1　This text is adapted from "Creative Sparks" by De Lange, C. (2012). *New Scientist*, January 14th.

galleries. And software has been built which creates art that could not have been imagined by the programmer.

2   Human beings are the only species to perform sophisticated creative acts regularly. If we can break this process down into computer code, where does that leave human creativity? "This is a question at the very core of humanity," says Geraint Wiggins, a computational creativity researcher at Goldsmiths, University of London. "It scares a lot of people. They are worried that it is taking something special away from what it means to be human."

3   To some extent, we are all familiar with computerized art. The question is: where does the work of the artist stop and the creativity of the computer begin? Consider one of the oldest machine artists, Aaron, a robot that has had paintings exhibited in London's Tate Modern and the San Francisco Museum of Modern Art. Aaron can pick up a paintbrush and paint on canvas on its own. **Impressive** perhaps, but it is still little more than a tool to realize the programmer's own creative ideas.

4   Simon Colton, the designer of the Painting Fool, is keen to make sure his creation doesn't attract the same criticism. Unlike earlier "artists", such as Aaron, the Painting Fool only needs minimal direction and can come up with its own concepts by going online for materials. The software runs its own web searches and **trawls** through social media sites. It is now beginning to display a kind of imagination too, creating pictures from scratch. One of its original works is a series of **fuzzy** landscapes, **depicting** trees and sky. While some might say they have a mechanical look, Colton argues that such reactions arise from people's double standards towards software-produced and human-produced art. After all, he says, consider that the Painting Fool painted the landscapes without referring to a photo. "If a child painted a new scene from its head, you'd say it has a certain level of imagination," he points out. "The same should be true of a machine." Software bugs can also lead to unexpected results. Some of the Painting Fool's paintings of a chair came out in black and white, thanks to a technical **glitch**. This gives the work an **eerie**, ghostlike quality. Human artists like the renowned Ellsworth Kelly are **lauded** for limiting their color **palette**—so why should computers be any different?

5   Researchers like Colton don't believe it is right to measure machine

creativity directly to that of humans who "have had **millennia** to develop our skills". Others, though, are fascinated by the prospect that a computer might create something as original and subtle as our best artists. So far, only one has come close. Composer David Cope[2] invented a program called Experiments in Musical Intelligence, or EMI[3]. Not only did EMI create compositions in Cope's style, but also that of the most **revered** classical composers, including Bach[4], Chopin[5], and Mozart[6]. Audiences were moved to tears, and EMI even fooled classical music experts into thinking they were hearing genuine Bach. Not everyone was impressed however. Some, such as Wiggins, have **blasted** Cope's work as **pseudoscience**, and condemned him for his **deliberately** vague explanation of how the software worked. Meanwhile, Douglas Hofstadter of Indiana University said EMI created **replicas** which still rely completely on the original artist's creative impulses. When audiences found out the truth they were often **outraged** with Cope, and one music lover even tried to punch him. Amid such controversy, Cope destroyed EMI's vital databases.

6   But why did so many people love the music, yet **recoil** when they discovered how it was composed? A study by computer scientist David Moffat of Glasgow Caledonian University provides a clue. He asked both expert musicians and non-experts to assess six compositions. The participants weren't told beforehand whether the tunes were composed by humans or computers, but were asked to guess, and then rate how much

---

2   David Cope: an American author, composer, scientist, and former professor of music at the University of California. His primary area of research involves artificial intelligence and music. He writes programs and algorithms that can analyze existing music and create new compositions in the style of the original input music.

3   EMI: In the 1980s, the composer and professor David Cope created a project called Experiments in Musical Intelligence (EMI). EMI was a computer program that analyzed the musical compositions of composers, such as Beethoven and Mozart, and could create a new composition that sounded as if the composer had written it.

4   Bach: Johann Sebastian Bach (1685–1750), a German composer, organist, and violinist of the Baroque Era. Bach wrote over eleven hundred music compositions in all genres.

5   Chopin: Frédéric Chopin (1810–1849), a Polish-born pianist and composer, was renowned as a leading musician of his era.

6   Mozart: Wolfgang Amadeus Mozart (1756–1791), a prolific Austrian composer. He created a string of operas, concertos, symphonies, and sonatas that are widely recognized as masterpieces of classical music.

they liked each one. People who thought the composer was a computer tended to dislike the piece more than those who believed it was human. This was true even among the experts, who might have been expected to be more objective in their analyses.

7 Where does this prejudice come from? Paul Bloom of Yale University has a suggestion: he **reckons** part of the pleasure we get from art **stems from** the creative process behind the work. This can give it an "irresistible essence", says Bloom. Meanwhile, experiments by Justin Kruger of New York University have shown that people's enjoyment of an artwork increases if they think more time and effort was needed to create it. Similarly, Colton thinks that when people experience art, they wonder what the artist might have been thinking or what the artist is trying to tell them. It seems obvious, therefore, that with computers producing art, this **speculation** is cut short—there's nothing to explore. But as technology becomes increasingly complex, finding those greater depths in computer art could become possible. This is precisely why Colton asks the Painting Fool to **tap into** online social networks for its inspiration: hopefully this way it will choose themes that will already be meaningful to us.

Words and Phrases

blast /blɑːst/ v. to criticize someone or something very strongly 抨击，严厉批评
e.g. The administration was blasted for failing to create jobs.

deliberately /dɪˈlɪbərətli/ adv. done in a way that is intended or planned 故意地
e.g. I'm sure he says these things deliberately to annoy me.

depict /dɪˈpɪkt/ v. to describe something or someone in writing or speech, or to show them in a painting, picture, etc. 描绘，描述
e.g. Her paintings depict the lives of ordinary people in the last century.

eerie /ˈɪəri/ adj. strange and frightening 怪异的；神秘的
e.g. He had the eerie feeling that he had met this stranger before.

Unit 2 Technology

enrapture	/ɪnˈræptʃə/	v.	to fill with great joy 使狂喜，使兴高采烈
		e.g.	The comedy is innocent enough for kids and weird enough to enrapture adults.
fuzzy	/ˈfʌzi/	adj.	unclear or confused 模糊的
		e.g.	The border between science fact and science fiction gets a bit fuzzy.
glitch	/glɪtʃ/	n.	a small fault in a machine or piece of equipment, that stops it working 小错误，过失
		e.g.	The system has been plagued with glitches ever since its launch.
impressive	/ɪmˈpresɪv/	adj.	something that is impressive makes you admire it because it is very good, large, important, etc. 给人留下深刻印象的；令人赞叹的
		e.g.	That was an impressive performance from such a young tennis player.
laud	/lɔːd/	v.	to praise someone or something 赞扬
		e.g.	The president lauded the rise of market economies around the world.
millennium	/mɪˈleniəm/	n.	(pl. millennia) a period of 1000 years 一千年，千周年
		e.g.	The year 2000 was celebrated as the beginning of the third millennium.
outraged	/ˈaʊtreɪdʒd/	adj.	feeling or showing anger 震怒的
		e.g.	He was outraged at the way he had been treated.
palette	/ˈpælət/	n.	a thin curved board that an artist uses to mix paints, holding it by putting his or her thumb through a hole at the edge 调色板
		e.g.	David Fincher paints from a palette consisting almost exclusively of grey and mud brown.
prestigious	/preˈstɪdʒəs/	adj.	admired as one of the best and most important 有声望的
		e.g.	Peking University is a prestigious university in China.
pseudoscience	/ˌsjuːdəʊˈsaɪəns/	n.	a system of thought or a theory that is not formed in a scientific way 伪科学
		e.g.	A pseudoscience is a set of ideas based on theories put forth as scientific when they are not scientific.

reckon	/ˈrekən/	v.	to think or suppose something 认为；把……看作
		e.g.	Children are reckoned to be more sophisticated nowadays.
recoil	/rɪˈkɔɪl/	v.	to move back suddenly and quickly from something you do not like or are afraid of 厌弃；强烈反对
		e.g.	People used to recoil from the idea of getting into debt.
replica	/ˈreplɪkə/	n.	an exact copy of something, especially a building, a gun, or a work of art 复制品；摹本
		e.g.	The city has estimated that it would cost $110,000 to raze the existing work and rebuild an exact replica.
revere	/rɪˈvɪə/	v.	to respect and admire someone or something very much 尊敬；崇敬
		e.g.	Today he's still revered as the father of the nation.
speculation	/ˌspekjəˈleɪʃən/	n.	when you guess about the possible causes or effects of something without knowing all the facts, or the guesses that you make 猜测；推断
		e.g.	There is speculation that the president is ill.
stem from			to develop as a result of something else 源自；由……造成
		e.g.	Their disagreement stemmed from a misunderstanding.
tap into			to manage to use something in a way that brings good results 利用，开发（已有的资源、知识等）
		e.g.	It is a great opportunity for us to tap into this newly developing market.
trawl	/trɔːl/	v.	to search through a lot of documents, lists, etc. in order to find out information 查阅，搜集
		e.g.	The software is used to trawl for information on the Internet.
trick	/trɪk/	v.	to deceive someone in order to get something from them or to make them do something 欺骗
		e.g.	John tricked the old lady into giving him eight hundred dollars.

Unit 2 Technology

Reading Comprehension

Task 1 Text A can be divided into the following three sections. Read the text carefully and work in pairs to find the main idea of each section. Then complete the following table.

Introduction (Para. 1)	• A great deal of progress has already been attained in this field of computer-produced art. 1) The Painting Fool, one of a growing number of computer programs, is claimed to possess _____. 2) Classical music by an artificial composer has brought people _____, and even made people believe that it is _____. 3) Artworks painted by a robot have sold for _____ and been hung in prestigious galleries.
People's responses to computerized art (Paras. 2–5)	• According to Geraint Wiggins, many people are worried about computer art because it _____. • Aron, one of the oldest machine artists, is considered little more than _____. • Simon Colton, the designer of _____, argues that people tend to judge computer art and human art by _____. • The controversy over Cope's EMI software: 1) David Cope's EMI software surprised people by generating work that was _____. 2) Wiggins criticized Cope's work as _____, and condemned him for not _____. 3) Douglas Hofstadter claimed that EMI was _____. 4) Audiences who had listened to EMI's music became angry after discovering that _____.
Reasons for people's different responses to computerized art (Paras. 6–7)	• The participants in David Moffat's study had to assess music without knowing _____. The study indicated that people who thought the composer was a computer tended to _____ more than those who believed it was human. • Paul Bloom of Yale University suggested that part of the pleasure we get from art stems from _____. • Justin Kruger's findings showed that _____ increases if they think more time and effort was needed to create it.

35

Task 2 Based on the information in Task 1, write a summary of the text in 80–100 words. Try to make your paragraph logical and coherent.

Task 3 Work in groups to discuss the following questions.

1. What are people's reactions towards the music composed by computers?
2. What are the findings of David Moffat's study?
3. Why do people have prejudice against computer art, according to the author?
4. How do you understand "people's double standards towards software-produced and human-produced art" in Para. 4?
5. What changes will computer-produced art bring to our life?

Vocabulary

Task 1 For each sentence there are four choices marked A, B, C, and D. Choose the one that best keeps the meaning with the underlined part.

1. There are some very <u>impressive</u> buildings in the town.

    A. striking   B. inconsistent   C. incredible   D. incompatible

2. Harvard University, which was founded in 1636 and has a long history of wealth and influence, is one of the most <u>prestigious</u> universities in the world.

    A. precious   B. famous   C. professional   D. private

3. News of the president's illness fueled <u>speculation</u> that an election will be held later in the year.

    A. peculiarity   B. spectacle   C. conjecture   D. prospect

4. Cupid is usually <u>depicted</u> as a winged boy with a bow and arrow.

    A. described   B. told   C. witnessed   D. distinguished

5. Nelson Mandela is <u>revered</u> for his brave fight against apartheid.

    A. rejected   B. respected   C. rewarded   D. awarded

Unit 2　**Technology**

6. We'd expect a few <u>glitches</u>, but everything's gone remarkably smoothly.

   A. accidents　　B. collapses　　C. problems　　D. calamities

7. Stephen is going to be pretty upset when he finds out how you <u>tricked</u> him.

   A. deceived　　B. treated　　C. ignored　　D. irritated

8. It is believed that the building was set on fire <u>deliberately</u>.

   A. apparently　　B. accidentally　　C. virtually　　D. intentionally

9. The basic facts of the story are starting to emerge though the details are still <u>fuzzy</u>.

   A. fussy　　B. unclear　　C. faulty　　D. fake

10. There was an <u>eerie</u> atmosphere throughout the afternoon.

    A. exciting　　B. exclusive　　C. strange　　D. enchanting

Task 2　Complete the following sentences with the words and expressions given below. Change the form if necessary.

outrage	enrapture	impressive	trawl
laud	blast	recoil	reckon
stem from	tap into		

1. The sale has been held up because the price is _____ to be too high.

2. She _____ from the idea of betraying her own brother.

3. Dickens was _____ for his social and moral sensitivity.

4. The irrational decision was _____ by environmental groups.

5. Reports of torture and mass executions in Serbia's detention camps have _____ the world's religious leaders.

6. All of us in the theater were _____ by the music.

7. She has a(n) _____ command of the English language.

8. You need to _____ through a lot of data to get results that are valid.

9. You are now a manager. It's up to you to figure out how to _____ and harness the talent around you.

10. Her problems _____ her difficult childhood.

Translation

Task 1 Translate the following paragraph into Chinese.

The Painting Fool is one of a growing number of computer programs which, so their makers claim, possess creative talents. Classical music by an artificial composer has had audiences enraptured, and even tricked them into believing a human was behind the score. Artworks painted by a robot have sold for thousands of dollars and been hung in prestigious galleries. And software has been built which creates art that could not have been imagined by the programmer.

_____

_____

Task 2 Translate the following paragraph into English with the help of the words in brackets.

当今社会对科学实验与创意表达相结合的需求日益迫切。数字化加速了艺术与科技的融合，为两者的结合提供了有利环境。计算机生成影像、动画和虚拟雕塑等"数字化艺术"利用数字化技术作为创意工具。知名公司 Apple 的联合创始人史蒂夫·乔布斯（Steve Jobs）擅长以艺术化的方式打造 Apple 设备，把计算机当作艺术作品。（tap into, prestigious, creative, reckon）

_____

_____

Information Theory—The Big Data
Read **Text B** and do the online exercises.

Summary Writing

Introduction

By summary, we mean a brief restatement, in your own words, of the content of a passage, an article, a chapter or a book. It is a condensed and objective account of the main ideas of a text. Usually, the length of a summary ranges between one and three paragraphs or 100 to 300 words, depending on the length and complexity of the original text and the intended audience and purpose. Writers should be clear about the purposes of the summary. The most common purposes for writing a summary include:

- showing that you have read and understood the original text;
- helping someone who has not read the text to understand the main idea;
- helping ourselves to generalize the main points of the text;
- arousing the interests of others.

Exercise 1 Have you ever written a summary before? Share within your group the purpose and content of your summary.

_____

_____

Organization of a Summary

A summary usually contains two parts: an introduction and the body. The introduction includes a thesis statement, which sums up the main point of the source. The body presents the main points without offering a personal opinion. There is actually no conclusion to your summary. Your essay will end once you have summarized the source text. Do not add your own concluding part unless you have some specific requirements or instructions from your teacher/professor. Below is the organization of a summary.

Introduction	<ul><li>Give the source title.</li><li>Provide the name of the author.</li><li>Present background information about the author or the text to be summarized.</li></ul>
Body	<ul><li>Include important data but omit minor points.</li><li>Include one or more of the author's examples, which can help bring your summary to life.</li><li>Do not include your own ideas or interpretations.</li></ul>

Features of a Summary

The primary purpose of a summary is to give an accurate, objective representation of the original work. As a general rule, you should not include your own ideas or interpretations. Typically, a summary will do the following:

- **Cite the author and title of the text.** In some cases, the place of publication or the context for the essay may also be included.
- **Indicate the main ideas of the text.** Accurately representing the main ideas (while omitting the less important details) is the major goal of the summary.
- **Use direct quotations of keywords, phrases, or sentences.** *Quote* the text directly for a few key ideas; *paraphrase* the other important ideas (that is, express the ideas in your own words).
- **Include author tags.** (e.g. "According to Barley" or "as Barley explains") to remind the reader that you are summarizing the author and the text, not giving your own ideas.
- **Avoid summarizing specific examples or data** unless they help illustrate the thesis or main idea of the text.
- **Report the main ideas as objectively as possible.** Do not include your reactions; save them for your response.

Exercise 2 Answer the questions about the features of a summary.

1. What information should be included in a summary?

   _____

   _____

2. How is a summary similar to or different from the original work?

   _____

   _____

Steps to Write a Summary

The following steps will be helpful when you are writing a summary:

1. Go over the text to find out the general theme.
2. Analyze the text's structure to divide it into several parts. Find out the main idea of each part and write it out briefly in your own words.
   - If you are summarizing a paragraph, you need to find out the topic sentence and the main supporting ideas of that paragraph.
   - If you are summarizing an essay, you need to find out the thesis statement, topic sentences of the body paragraphs, and the main supporting ideas.
3. Write down the key supporting points for each main idea without involving minor details.
4. Organize the main ideas and related supporting points in a logical order with necessary transitions and signal words to achieve coherence.
5. Reread the original work and proofread your summary.
   - Check to see that you have included only the main idea(s).
   - Check the wording of the summary to see that you did not use too many of the same words used in the original text.
   - Check that you did not include your opinion in the summary.

Exercise 3 Find out some useful transitions in summary writing.

_____

_____

Samples of Summary Writing

A. **One-Paragraph Summary**

A representative sample of language, compiled for the purpose of linguistic analysis, is known as a corpus. A corpus enables the linguist to make unbiased statements about frequency of usage, and it provides accessible data for the use of different researchers. Its range and size are variable. Some corpora attempt to cover the language as a whole, taking extracts from many kinds of text; others are extremely selective, providing a collection of material that deals only with a particular linguistic feature. The size of the corpus depends on practical factors, such as the time available to collect, process and store the data: it can take up to several hours to provide an accurate transcription of a few minutes of speech. Sometimes a small sample of data will be enough to decide a linguistic hypothesis; by contrast, corpora in major research projects can total millions of words. An important principle is that all corpora, whatever their size, are inevitably limited in their coverage, and always need to be supplemented by data derived from the intuitions of native speakers of the language, through either introspection or experimentation.

Exercise 4 Complete the summary of the following paragraph with no more than three words in each blank.

A linguist can use a corpus to comment objectively on _____. Some corpora include a wide range of language while others are used to focus on a _____. The length of time the process takes will affect the _____ of the corpus. No corpus can ever cover the whole language and so linguists often find themselves relying on the additional information that can be gained from the _____ of those who speak the language concerned.

B. **Multi-Paragraph Summary**

Visual Learning. Visual learners learn best when they can see information either in written language or in a picture or design. These learners also may need to see a teacher's nonverbal communication (body language and facial expressions) to fully understand the content of a lesson. In a classroom visual learners benefit from instructors who use a blackboard (or whiteboard) or an overhead projector to list important points of a lecture or use visual aids such as films, videos, maps, and charts. In addition, visual learners may learn best from class notes and outlines or pictures and diagrams in textbooks. They may also like to study by themselves in a quiet room and may visualize a picture of something or see information in their mind when trying to remember it.

Auditory Learning. Auditory learners learn best when they can hear information or when they are learning in an oral language format. In a classroom these learners benefit most from listening to lectures or participating in group discussions. Auditory learners may also read text aloud or use audiotapes or CDs to obtain information. When trying to remember something, these learners can often "hear" the information the way someone told it to them or the way they previously repeated it out loud. In general, these people learn best when interacting with others in a listening/speaking exchange.

Tactile/Kinesthetic Learning. Tactile/kinesthetic learners like to be physically engaged in hands-on activities or to actively explore the physical world around them. In the classroom they benefit from a lab setting, where they can manipulate materials to learn new information. These people learn best when they can be physically active in their learning environment. They may find it difficult to sit in one place for long periods of time, and they may also become distracted by their need to be exploring and active. Tactile/kinesthetic learners benefit most from instructors who encourage in-class demonstrations, hands-on learning experiences, and field work outside the classroom.

Exercise 5 Here are two summaries of the above three paragraphs. Read each of the summaries and decide which of the following problem(s) it has.

A. The summary uses too many of the same words as the original text.
B. The summary is too short.

C. The summary is too long and contains too many details.

D. The summary does not contain all the main ideas.

Summary 1

The three learning styles are visual, auditory, and tactile/kinesthetic and each is related to a different sense. The visual style is related what the learner can see and visualize in his or her head. The auditory style involves listening and speaking.

Summary 2

The three learning styles are visual, auditory, and tactile/kinesthetic; each is related to a different sense. The visual style is related to what the learner can see. Visual learners learn best from information in writing and on charts, pictures, and other visual aids. These learners do well in a class where the teacher uses a lot of body language and facial expressions as well as a whiteboard or blackboard and visual technology such as overhead projectors and videos. The auditory style involves listening and speaking. Auditory learners like to hear information presented on tapes or in lectures, and they learn best when they can interact verbally with others. They like to participate in discussions either with a group or with a partner. The tactile/kinesthetic style is related to the sense of touch or to body movement. Learners strong in this style like to actively participate in their learning and enjoy hands-on experiences both inside and outside the classroom. Because they can get bored easily by sitting in one place, they need to take field trips, work in lab settings, and use their hands.

Exercise 6 Write a summary for these three paragraphs in your own words.

_____
_____
_____
_____
_____

Writing Practice

Task   *Read the text below and write a summary of it.*

At the beginning of this chapter, we looked at the various roles of language in our lives: thinking, sharing information, persuading others, interacting socially, etc. When we look at all the ways we use language, we tend to focus on the many positive opportunities that language gives us.

However, as we have seen with sense perception, language also has its problems and limitations as a way of knowing.

- Language is not always precise.
- There are many languages in the world and meaning can be lost in translation.
- There are experiences which cannot be expressed using language.

In spite of these limitations, language is one of the most important ways of knowing. It is our main means of building a bridge between personal knowledge and shared knowledge. Because of language, we are not isolated in our own thoughts; we are able to connect with others both socially and culturally.

Indeed, it could be said that the same features of language that we have highlighted as problems can also be seen as the things which make language so wonderfully human and different.

- Lack of precision and misunderstanding can lead to deeper enquiry, as well as to humour.
- The existence of different languages helps us to discover new ways of interpreting experiences.
- Language can be used by poets and writers to communicate ideas and feelings that others find difficult to express.

Language is the tool with which we claim knowledge and often the tool with which we share knowledge. We can gain knowledge using this tool, but we need to be aware of its limitations. In particular, we must be aware of the influence that the language user's perspective has on the knowledge that is transmitted.

Source: Dombrowski, E., Rotenberg, L., & Bick, M. (2013). *Theory of Knowledge: Course Companion* (2nd ed.). Oxford: Oxford University Press.

UNIT 3
Economy

Introduction

In the economic activities, managers and marketing play a vital role. Failing to realize the major trends and to put to use marketing strategies means missed profit opportunities. How to conduct a market research? How to become skillful at analyzing and exploiting trends? And how much do you know about doctoring sales? Text A and B in this unit will uncover the veils of these questions and help you get a glimpse of the maze of market strategies.

Learning Objectives

Reading

- Understanding the strategies of analyzing and exploiting trends
- Identifying the essay structure of a business review
- Summarizing the main ideas using topic-related words or phrases
- Developing your own ideas about doctoring sales

Writing

- Understanding the features of an abstract
- Knowing the structure of an abstract
- Identifying different types of abstracts
- Writing an abstract

Unit 3 Economy

Text A

🎓 Topic Exploration

Step 1 Conduct a research on how trends affect people's perception about the world around them.

Step 2 Work in groups to discuss the benefits and harms of going with the tide, and prepare an oral report to the whole class.

🎓 Reading

Making the Most of Trends[1]

Experts from Harvard Business School give advice to managers.

1 Most managers can identify the major trends of the day. But in the course of conducting research in a number of industries and working directly with companies, we have discovered that managers often fail to recognize the less obvious but profound ways these trends are influencing consumers' aspirations, attitudes, and behaviors. This is especially true of trends that managers view as **peripheral** to their core markets.

2 Many ignore trends in their innovation strategies or adopt a wait-and-see approach and let competitors take the lead. At a minimum, such responses mean missed profit opportunities. At the extreme,

---

1 This text is adapted from "Are You Ignoring Trends That Could Shake up Your Business?" by Ofek, E., & Wathieu, L. (2010). *Harvard Business Review*, 88 (7–8), 124–131.

they can **jeopardize** a company by **ceding** to rivals the opportunity to transform the industry. The purpose of this article is twofold: to **spur** managers to think more expansively about how trends could **engender** new value **propositions** in their core markets, and to provide some high-level advice on how to make market research and product development personnel more **adept at** analyzing and exploiting trends.

3 One strategy, known as "**infuse** and **augment**", is to design a product or service that retains most of the **attributes** and functions of existing products in the category but adds others that address the needs and desires **unleashed** by a major trend. A case in point is the Poppy range of handbags, which the firm Coach[2] created in response to the economic **downturn** of 2008. The Coach brand had been a symbol of **opulence** and luxury for nearly 70 years, and the most obvious reaction to the downturn would have been to lower prices. However, that would have risked cheapening the brand's image. Instead, they initiated a consumer-research project which revealed that customers were eager to lift themselves and the country out of tough times. Using these insights, Coach launched the lower-priced Poppy handbags, which were in vibrant colors, and looked more youthful and playful than conventional Coach products. Creating the sub-brand allowed Coach to **avert** an across-the-board price cut. In contrast to the many companies that responded to the recession by cutting prices, Coach saw the new consumer **mindset** as an opportunity for innovation and **renewal**.

4 A further example of this strategy was supermarket Tesco's[3] response to consumers' growing concerns about the environment. With that in mind, Tesco, one of the world's top five retailers, introduced its Greener Living program, which demonstrates the company's **commitment** to protecting the environment by involving consumers in ways that produce **tangible** results. For example, Tesco customers can accumulate points for such activities as reusing bags, recycling cans and printer **cartridges**,

---

2 Coach: also known as Coach New York, an American company specializing in luxury accessories such as handbags. It was founded in 1941 as a family-run workshop.

3 Tesco: founded in 1919, a British multinational groceries and general merchandise retailer with headquarters in Welwyn Garden City, Hertfordshire, England, United Kingdom.

and buying home-**insulation** materials. Like points earned on regular purchases, these green points can be **redeemed** for cash. Tesco has not abandoned its traditional retail offerings but augmented its business with these innovations, thereby infusing its value proposition with a green **streak**.

5   A more radical strategy is "combine and transcend". This entails combining aspects of the product's existing value proposition with attributes addressing changes arising from a trend, to create a novel experience—one that may land the company in an entirely new market space. At first glance, spending resources to incorporate elements of a seemingly irrelevant trend into one's core offerings sounds like it's hardly worthwhile. But consider Nike's move to integrate the digital revolution into its reputation for high-performance athletic footwear. In 2006, they **teamed up** with technology company Apple to launch Nike+, a digital sports kit comprising a sensor that attaches to the running shoe and a wireless receiver that connects to the user's iPod. By combining Nike's original value proposition for amateur athletes with one for digital consumers, the Nike+ sports kit and web interface moved the company from a focus on athletic **apparel** to a new plane of engagement with its customers.

6   A third approach, known as "counteract and reaffirm", involves developing products or services that stress the values traditionally associated with the category in ways that allow consumers to oppose— or at least temporarily escape from—the aspects of trends they view as undesirable. A product that accomplished this is the ME2[4], a video game created by Canada's iToys. By reaffirming the toy category's association with physical play, the ME2 counteracted some of the widely perceived negative impacts of digital gaming devices. Like other handheld games, the device featured a host of exciting interactive games, a full-color LCD screen, and advanced 3D graphics. What set it apart was that it incorporated the traditional physical component of children's play: it contained a **pedometer**, which tracked and awarded points for physical activity (walking, running, biking, skateboarding, climbing stairs). The child could use the points to enhance various virtual skills needed for

---

4   ME2: Mass Effect 2, the second game in the Mass Effect triology. It is a role-playing action video game developed by BioWare and published by Electronic Arts.

the video game. The ME2, introduced in mid-2008, **catered to** kids' huge desire to play video games while countering the negatives, such as associations with lack of exercise and obesity.

7 Once you have gained perspective on how trend-related changes in consumer opinions and behaviors impact on your category, you can determine which of our three innovation strategies to pursue. When your category's basic value proposition continues to be meaningful for consumers influenced by the trend, the infuse-and-augment strategy will allow you to **reinvigorate** the category. If analysis reveals an increasing **disparity** between your category and consumers' new focus, your innovations need to transcend the category to integrate the two worlds. Finally, if aspects of the category **clash with** undesired outcomes of a trend, such as associations with unhealthy lifestyles, there is an opportunity to counteract those changes by reaffirming the core values of your category.

8 Trends—technological, economic, environmental, social, or political—that affect how people perceive the world around them and shape what they expect from products and services present firms with unique opportunities for growth.

Words and Phrases

adept at			good at something that needs care and skill 熟练的；擅长的
		e.g.	He is adept at cutting through red tape.
apparel	/ə'pærəl/	*n.*	clothing 服装
		e.g.	Only under the premise of the talents and interests can they succeed in apparel design industry.
attribute	/'ætrəbju:t/	*n.*	a quality or feature, especially one that is considered to be good or useful 属性，特性；品质
		e.g.	Kindness is an attribute of a good teacher.
augment	/ɔ:g'ment/	*v.*	to increase the value, amount, effectiveness, etc. of something 增大；增加
		e.g.	Her secretarial work helped to augment the family's income.

Unit 3 Economy

avert /əˈvɜːt/   *v.*   to prevent something unpleasant from happening 防止；避免
- *e.g.* Talks will be held today in a final attempt to avert strike action.

cartridge /ˈkɑːtrɪdʒ/   *n.*   a small container or piece of equipment that you put inside something to make it work 打印机的墨盒；相机的暗盒；弹药筒
- *e.g.* The printer needs a new ink cartridge.

cater to   try to satisfy (a particular need or demand) 迎合，设法满足（需要）
- *e.g.* They only publish novels which cater to the mass market.

cede /siːd/   *v.*   to give something such as an area of land or a right to a country or person, especially when you are forced to 放弃（权力）；割让（领土）
- *e.g.* They have had to cede ground to the government.

clash with   (two opinions, statements, or qualities) differ greatly from each other 与……对抗/冲突
- *e.g.* Don't make any policy decisions that clash with official company thinking.

commitment /kəˈmɪtmənt/   *n.*   the hard work and loyalty that someone gives to an organization, activity, etc. 献身；投入
- *e.g.* I was impressed by the energy and commitment shown by the players.

disparity /dɪˈspærəti/   *n.*   a difference between two or more things, especially an unfair one 悬殊；巨大差异
- *e.g.* The arrangements could lead to disparity of treatment between companies.

downturn /ˈdaʊntɜːn/   *n.*   a period or process in which business activity, production, etc. is reduced and conditions become worse（经济、商业等活动的）回落，下降趋势
- *e.g.* There has been a downturn in the housing market since last autumn.

engender /ɪnˈdʒendə/   *v.*   to be the cause of a situation or feeling 造成；引起，产生
- *e.g.* The issue engendered continuing controversy.

infuse /ɪnˈfjuːz/   *v.*   to fill something or someone with a particular feeling or quality 注满；充满
- *e.g.* Her work is infused with an anger born of pain and oppression.

insulation	/ˌɪnsjəˈleɪʃən/	n.	material used to insulate something, especially a building 绝缘；隔离；隔绝
		e.g.	Keep your home warmer through insulation.
jeopardize	/ˈdʒepədaɪz/	v.	to risk losing or spoiling something important 使处于危险境地；损害
		e.g.	A devaluation of the dollar would jeopardize New York's position as a financial center.
mindset	/ˈmaɪndset/	n.	someone's general attitude, and the way in which they think about things and make decisions 思想倾向；精神状态；心态
		e.g.	The company seems to have a very old-fashioned mindset.
opulence	/ˈɒpjələns/	n.	the total of one's money and property 富裕；豪华
		e.g.	His eyes had never beheld such opulence.
pedometer	/pəˈdɒmətə/	n.	an instrument that measures how far you walk 计步器
		e.g.	The easiest way to measure distance is to get hold of a pedometer.
peripheral	/pəˈrɪfərəl/	adj.	not as important as other things or people in a particular activity, idea, or situation 次要的，无关紧要的
		e.g.	She will see their problems as peripheral to her own.
proposition	/ˌprɒpəˈzɪʃən/	n.	a suggestion, or something that is suggested or considered as a possible thing to do 提议；建议；主张
		e.g.	He wrote to me last week regarding a business proposition he thought might interest me.
redeem	/rɪˈdiːm/	v.	to exchange a piece of paper representing an amount of money for that amount of money or for goods equal in cost to that amount of money 赎回，买回；兑换（物品、折扣或现金）
		e.g.	You can redeem the coupon at any store.
reinvigorate	/riːɪnˈvɪgəreɪt/	v.	to put new strength or power into something 给……以新的活力，使恢复元气
		e.g.	We are fully committed to reinvigorating the economy of the area.
renewal	/rɪˈnjuːəl/	n.	a situation in which something is replaced, improved or made more successful 更新；改进

		e.g.	The desire for innovation and renewal applies to many areas in life and work.
spur	/spɜː/	v.	to encourage someone or make them want to do something 激励；鼓励
		e.g.	Her son's passion for computer games spurred her on to set up a software shop.
streak	/striːk/	n.	a part of someone's character that is different from the rest of their character 特征；倾向
		e.g.	The libertarian streak of the Austrians still has its fans.
tangible	/ˈtændʒəbəl/	adj.	clear enough or definite enough to be easily seen or noticed 可触摸的，明确的；真实的
		e.g.	The atmosphere of neglect and abandonment was almost tangible.
team up			to join with someone in order to work on something 协作；配合
		e.g.	He teamed up with the band to produce a disc.
unleash	/ʌnˈliːʃ/	v.	to suddenly let a strong force, feeling, etc. have its full effect 放开；释放
		e.g.	The announcement unleashed a storm of protest from the public.

Reading Comprehension

Task 1 Text A can be divided into the following three sections. Read the text carefully and work in pairs to find the main idea of each section. Then complete the following table.

Introduction (Paras. 1–2)	• Most managers can identify the major trends of the day. But they cannot recognize _____ these trends are influencing consumers' _____, _____, and _____. • Those trends that are seen as _____ are often ignored by managers. • The purposes of this article: to encourage manager _____; _____ on how to make market research and product development personnel more skillful at analyzing and exploiting trends.

Strategies **(Paras. 3–7)**	• Advice given by experts: 1) Strategy One: _____. Tesco's response to _____ is a good example. 2) Strategy Two: _____. Nike+ sports kit and web interface moved the company to a _____. 3) Strategy Three: _____. A video game, ME2, accomplished this. The ME2 satisfied kids' demand to _____ _____ and at the same time _____, for example, associations with lack of exercise and obesity. • Trends impact on customers and have changed their _____ _____.
Conclusion **(Para. 8)**	• Trends in _____ affect how people look at the world and determine what they hope to get from products and services.

Task 2 Based on the information in Task 1, write a summary of the text in 80–100 words. Try to make your paragraph logical and coherent.

Task 3 Work in groups to discuss the following questions.

1. How did Coach cope with the economic downturn of 2008?

2. How did Nike introduce digital revolution into its high-performance athletic footwear?

3. How do you understand "trends present firms with unique opportunities for growth"?

4. Who lead the market trend, the customers or the products?

5. In what ways are trends influencing consumers' aspirations, attitudes, and behaviors?

Vocabulary

Task 1 For each sentence there are four choices marked A, B, C, and D. Choose the one that best keeps the meaning with the underlined part.

1. She was forced to try and <u>augment</u> her earnings by taking on a cleaning job in the evenings.

    A. increase   B. enrich   C. measure   D. extend

2. For most people, there is a great disparity between their intrinsic value and the compensation they receive for their efforts.

   A. disadvantage   B. difference   C. distraction   D. disposal

3. It is impossible to prove that watching violent films engenders violence among children.

   A. entrusts   B. engages   C. causes   D. enforces

4. She knew that by failing her finals she could jeopardize her whole future.

   A. risk   B. manipulate   C. constrain   D. intimidate

5. The issue of subsidies is peripheral to the question of agricultural reform.

   A. superior   B. prior   C. secondary   D. conducive

6. The arrival of a group of friends on Saturday infused new life into the weekend.

   A. imposed   B. inflicted   C. injected   D. encouraged

7. The tax relief was important to spur consumption and investment to get us out of this recession.

   A. inspire   B. promote   C. generate   D. increase

8. Internet shopping caters to every conceivable need.

   A. satisfies   B. provides   C. affords   D. contributes

9. He managed to avert the closure of the factory.

   A. divert   B. invert   C. convert   D. avoid

10. The officers were still reluctant to unleash their troops in pursuit of a defeated enemy.

    A. lead   B. arrange   C. send   D. distribute

Task 2 Complete the following sentences with the words and phrases given below. Change the form if necessary.

redeem	vibrant	tangible	downturn
spur	jeopardize	clash with	adept at
team up	integrate into		

1. In fact, it is essential that law librarians strive to become _____ using government documents.

2. Companies increasingly want to see _____ benefits from their investment in technology.

3. The room was painted in a series of _____ orange, red and yellow stripes.

4. In 1988, the SDP _____ with the Liberal Party, forming the Liberal Democratic Party.

5. Any renewal of the violence will _____ the success of the peace negotiations.

6. She managed to save enough money to _____ her jewellery from the pawn shop.

7. All the department reports should _____ one annual statement.

8. At this point, his family responsibilities _____ his career plans and a choice had to be made.

9. It was an article in the local newspaper which finally _____ him into action.

10. The country's economy has taken a(n) _____ because of the economic crisis.

Translation

Task 1 Translate the following paragraph into Chinese.

Many ignore trends in their innovation strategies or adopt a wait-and-see approach and let competitors take the lead. At a minimum, such responses mean missed profit opportunities. At the extreme, they can jeopardize a company by ceding to rivals the opportunity to transform the industry. The purpose of this article is twofold: to spur managers to think more expansively about how trends could engender new value propositions in their core markets, and to provide some high-level advice on how to make market research and product development personnel more adept at analyzing and exploiting trends.

Task 2 *Translate the following paragraph into English with the help of the words in brackets.*

数字化产品和服务在消费者的日常生活中发挥着愈加重要的作用，经济衰退让人们的消费行为更加谨慎，公众对全球变暖的担忧影响着购买决策。你是否注意到这些趋势背后更深层次的含义？你是否发现，长期的衰退引发的不是痼疾，而是激发出一种需要提升和激励的愿望？（major, recession, unleash, lift）

Doctoring Sales

Read **Text B** online and do the exercises.

Writing an Abstract

Introduction

An abstract is simply a short, stand-alone summary of the work or paper that readers can use as an overview. Even though an abstract goes at the beginning of the work, it acts as a summary of the entire paper. It describes what the writer does in the essay, whether it's a scientific experiment or a literary analysis paper.

A well-written abstract serves multiple purposes:

- To make readers get the gist or essence of the paper quickly so as to decide whether to read the full paper;
- To prepare readers to follow the detailed information, analyses, and arguments in the full paper;
- To help readers remember key points of the paper.

Exercise 1 Have you ever written an abstract before? Share within your group the purpose and the content of your abstract.

_____

_____

Types of Abstracts

There are basically two types of abstracts: descriptive abstract and informative abstract. Typically, descriptive abstracts are best for shorter papers while informative abstracts are used for much longer and technical research.

	Descriptive abstract	Informative abstract
Content	explain the purpose, research methods briefly	an overview of the paper including the purpose, research methods, results, conclusion
Length	within 100–200 words	a single paragraph, or several paragraphs
Use	in shorter papers	in longer and technical papers

Exercise 2 Read the two abstracts below and answer the following questions.

Abstract 1

This paper presents an analysis of the principles of magnetic refrigeration with application to air conditioning. A comparison with conventional evaporation-condensation gas cycle device is presented. Conclusions concerning the applicability of magnetic refrigeration to air conditioning are made.

Abstract 2

This paper explores the history of one company and its bid for survival in the rapidly changing world of today. It examines the plastics industry in America and the position of the company within it, detailing the growth of the company over the past 50 years and the expansion of the product range and facilities to the present time. The philosophy of management is explained and related to other industrialized countries. Consideration is given to possible future trends and the direction the company should now take in the light of world and local developments.

1. Which type(s) of abstract does the two abstracts belong to?

_____

_____

2. What differences can you find between the two abstracts?

_____

_____

Features of an Abstract

An effective abstract should:
- be able to stand alone;
- avoid repetition;
- use one well-developed, unified, coherent and concise paragraph of no more than 250 words;
- use the third person;
- use the passive voice;
- present the research purpose, methods, results, conclusion and recommendations;
- add no new information, but simply summarize the paper.

Exercise 3 What other features do you think an effective abstract should have?

_____

_____

Format of an Abstract

There are specific questions an abstract must provide answers for, but the answers must be kept in order as well. Ideally, it should be consistent with the overall format of an essay, with a general introduction, body, and conclusion.

The table below shows the usual structure for an abstract:

Introduction	<ul><li>Include a brief overview of the problem and its causes.</li><li>Indicate the purpose/objective of the study.</li><li>State the importance/significance of the study.</li></ul>
Body	<ul><li>Describe the methods used.</li><li>State main findings or results.</li></ul>
conclusion	<ul><li>Give conclusions based on findings.</li><li>Provide implications of the study.</li></ul>

Exercise 4 Find out the words which tell the research purpose, methods, and results in the following abstract.

Roads constructed of conventional pavement are subject to deformation after prolonged use. Laboratory model study of an anchored pavement was carried out. The objective of the study was to investigate construction problems and to develop specifications for a full-scale test. The study compared 1/20 scale anchored pavement and conventional slabs of similar dimensions. The model test results were compared with results from finite-element analysis. The deformations were lower for the anchored pavement compared with those for the conventional slab, and stresses in the soil were reduced and distributed more widely by rigid anchors. These findings indicate that an anchored slab offers distinct advantages over a conventional slab. The ANSYS computer program could be used to analyze such a soil-structure system, incorporating the environmental and mechanical effects.

Steps to Write an Abstract

1. Clarify the research purpose

You may start writing an abstract by clearly defining the purpose of your research. First, you can include a brief overview of the problem and explain why the problem is worth researching. After that, you need to state the purpose or objective of your research. Use verbs like *investigate*, *test*, *analyze* or *evaluate* to describe exactly what you set out to do. This section should also include the importance or significance of your work and the impact it might have if successful.

Research purpose can be written in the present or past simple tense, but should never refer to the future, as the research has already been completed.

This study will investigate the relationship between bilingual education and language learning. (×)

This study investigates the relationship between bilingual education and language learning. (√)

2. Explain the research methods

The methods section focuses on how you completed your research. The goal is to give readers an overview of the overall approach and procedures your research used. In this part, you need to discuss the kind of data you gathered and your methods of data collection. You also need to include the respondents of your study, as well as their population number. That is to say, the explanation of your methods should be brief and concise, and it also needs to be specific.

Research methods are usually written in the past simple tense as it refers to completed actions. Look at the following examples:

Surveys will be conducted with 15 participants. (×)

Surveys were conducted with 65 participants. (√)

3. Describe the research results

The results section is a brief summary of your main findings. It provides the answer to research questions. In this part, you need to highlight only the most important findings that will allow the reader to understand your conclusions. Depending on how complex your research is, you may not be able to include all results here.

Research results can be written in the present or past simple tense. Look at the following examples:

Our analysis has shown a strong correlation between coffee consumption and productivity. (×)

Our analysis shows a strong correlation between coffee consumption and productivity. (√)

Our analysis showed a strong correlation between coffee consumption and productivity. (√)

4. Conclude the research implications

The conclusion section is a summary as well as a closure of the abstract. It addresses the conclusion as well as implications of your study. In this part, you need to explain what your findings mean and why they make your paper important. You may also include recommendations for implementation if your aim was to solve a practical problem.

Conclusions are usually written in the present simple tense. Look at the following examples:

We concluded that bilingual education enhances language learning. (×)

The results of the study clearly indicate that bilingual education enhances language learning. (√)

Exercise 5 Below is a random list of sentences of an abstract. Put them in correct order to make it a well-structured abstract.

_____ (a) In addition, most students in the CW condition found the experience enjoyable and felt that it contributed to their L2 learning.

_____ (b) Results of the study showed that CW had an overall significant effect on students' L2 writing; however, this effect varied from one writing skill area to another. Specifically, the effect was significant for content, organization, and vocabulary, but not for grammar or mechanics.

_____ (c) This study investigated the effectiveness and students' perceptions of collaborative writing (CW) in second language (L2).

_____ (d) A number of theoretical and pedagogical implications of the study, and limitations and directions for further research, are presented.

_____ (e) The study involved 38 first year students in two intact classes at a large university in the UAE (United Arab Emirates). One class consisted of 18 students and was considered the experimental group, and the second consisted of 20 students and was considered the control group. In the control group, writing tasks were carried out by students individually; in the experimental group, these tasks were carried out in pairs.

_____ (f) Writing quality was determined by a holistic rating procedure that included content, organization, grammar, vocabulary, and mechanics.

_____ (g) Results of the study are discussed in light of the social constructivist perspective of learning.

_____ (h) The study lasted 16 weeks and involved a pre- and post-test.

Sample Abstract Analysis

Feedback and assessment play an important role in teaching and learning of oral presentation skills. This study describes the implementation and evaluation of an innovative instruction that uses a Student Response System for peer assessment of oral presentations. A large number of oral presentations were assessed and students' perceptions and learning progress concerning the particular instructional approach were investigated. Results showed that the Student Response System was an effective way to produce feedback for presenters, assessors and educators. Results also revealed a very positive students' attitude towards the instructional format. The learning effect concerning assessment was rather limited. Further research is needed to come to conclusive statements about the latter.

Exercise 6 Read the abstract above and answer the following questions.

1. Complete the table with suitable key words or phrases from the above abstract.

Purpose	
Methods	
Results	
Conclusion	
Implications	

2. Analyze the features of the above abstract and answer the following questions.

1) Objectivity is an important feature of an abstract. What ways are used to make the abstract objective? Explain with examples.

2) What ways are used to make the abstract coherent? Identify the words or phrases which help achieve coherence.

Writing Practice

Task Write an abstract of an academic paper on your major. Refer to the guidelines and techniques for abstract writing. Keep in mind the qualities of a good abstract.

UNIT 4
Society

Introduction

Thanks to the development of modern science and technology, people live a more convenient and faster life than ever. It is reported that we have more and more aging population now. Due to longevity, late marriage and more divorces, the consensus of traditional families have given way to a myriad of family styles. Many young couples get together quickly but depart very soon. Some people say this is the side effect of information technology and the Internet, which provide more ways for people to make new friends online. Are there any other reasons? Have you ever imagined your life after retirement? In this unit, the two texts will tell you more about marriage and family.

Learning objectives

Reading

- Knowing various family styles in modern society
- Cultivating correct family values and sense of social responsibility
- Identifying the essay structure of a social study
- Finding out reasons for divorce and solutions to the aging problem

Writing

- Understanding the features of a problem-solution essay
- Knowing the similarities and differences between two formats of a problem-solution essay
- Learning to choose the suitable format when writing a problem-solution essay
- Using solid evidence to argue the feasibility of a solution

Unit 4　Society

Text A

Topic Exploration

Step 1　Conduct an interview with your parents and other elderly relatives to learn their ideas about marriage and divorce. Then talk with your friends or classmates to know their opinions on marriage and divorce.

Step 2　Compare your interview results with those of your group members, and then summarize your findings in two aspects:
- the similarities and differences of views on marriage and divorce between the two generations
- reasons for the differences

Step 3　Report your summary to the whole class.

Reading

Divorce: A Love Story[1]

*While the government talks up family values, marriage break-ups are **soaring**.*

1　Yang Yourong's wife kicks him as they walk upstairs and he falls back a few steps, then follows again at a distance up to the **cramped** offices of a district-government bureau handling divorces in Chongqing, a region in the southwest of China. After more than 20 years of marriage, Mr.

1　This text is adapted from "Divorce: A Love Story". (2016). *The Economist*, January 23rd.

Yang's wife has had several affairs; she is "quick tempered", he says (she had slapped him earlier, he claims). At the bureau, divorce takes half an hour and costs 9 yuan ($1.40). It is administered a few steps away from where other couples get married and take **celebratory** photographs. Mr. Yang and his wife have second thoughts, however; they return home, still arguing. Most couples hesitate less.

2   Divorce rates are rising quickly across China. This is a remarkable transformation in a society where for centuries marriage was universal and mostly permanent (though convention permitted men to take concubines). Traditional values have retained a strong influence over family relationships: during much of the Mao era, divorce was very unusual. It became more common in the 1980s, but a marriage law adopted in 1994 still required a reference from an employer or community leader. Not until 2003 were restrictions removed.

3   The trend reflects profound economic and social change. In the past 35 years, the biggest internal migration experienced by any country in human history has been tearing families apart. Traditional values have been giving way to more liberal ones. Women are becoming better educated, and more aware of their marital rights (they now initiate over half of all divorce cases). Greater affluence has made it easier for many people to **contemplate** living alone—no longer is there such an incentive to stay married in order to **pool** resources.

4   As long as both sides agree on terms, China is now among the easiest and cheapest places in the world to get a divorce. In many Western countries, including Britain, couples must separate for a period before **dissolving** a marriage; China has no such constraints. In 2014, the latest year for which such data exist, about 3.6 million couples split up—more than double the number

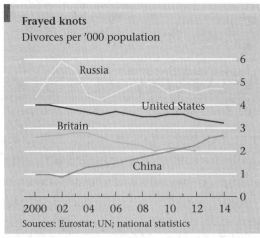

Economist.com

a decade earlier (they received a red certificate, pictured, to prove it). The divorce rate—the number of cases per thousand people—also doubled in that period. It now stands at 2.7, well above the rate in most of Europe and approaching that of America, the most divorce-prone Western country (see chart). Chongqing's rate, 4.4, is higher than America's.

5   Helped by the huge movement of people from the countryside into cities, and the rapid spread of social media, the availability of potential mates has grown with astonishing speed, both geographically and virtually. But many migrants marry in their home villages and often live apart from their spouses for lengthy periods. This has contributed to a big increase in extramarital liaisons. Married people previously had limited opportunities to meet members of the opposite sex in social situations, according to research by Li Xiaomin of Henan University. Peng Xiaobo, a divorce lawyer in Chongqing, reckons 60%–70% of his clients have had affairs.

6   Such behavior has led to much soul-searching. The notion that "chopsticks come in pairs"[2] is still prevalent; propaganda posters preach Confucian[3]-style family virtues using pictures of happy, multi-generation families. Many commentators in the official media talk of separation as a sign of moral failure; they **fret** that it signifies the decline of marriage, and of family as a social unit—a threat, as they see it, to social stability and even a cause of crime. The spread of "Western values" is often blamed.

7   But marriage is not losing its **luster**. In most countries, rising divorce rates coincide with more births out of wedlock and a fall in marriage rates. China **bucks** both these trends. Remarriage is common too. The Chinese have not fallen out of love with marriage—only with each other.

8   It is tradition itself that is partly to blame for rising divorce rates. China's legal marriage age for men, 22, is the highest in the world. But conservative attitudes to premarital relationships result in Chinese youths

---

2 chopsticks come in pairs: "A pair of chopsticks" bears Chinese people's feelings and memory, showing chopsticks as a symbol of love.

3 Confucian: of Confucius. Confucius is one of the most famous people in ancient China, a wise philosopher on moralities and human behavior. He is also a great educator with many famous sayings on education.

having fewer of them than their counterparts in the West (they are urged to concentrate on their studies and careers, rather than socialize or explore). Living together before marriage is still rare, although that is changing among educated youngsters. People still face social pressure to marry in their 20s. Their inexperience makes it more than usually difficult for them to select a good partner.

9   Couples' ageing relatives are part of the problem too. Yan Yunxiang of the University of California, Los Angeles, says "parent-driven divorce" is becoming more common. As a result of China's one-child-per-couple policy (recently changed to a two-child one), many people have no siblings to share the burden of looking after parents and grandparents. Thus, couples often find themselves living with, or being watched over by, several—often contending—elders. Mr. Yan says the older ones' interference **fuels conjugal** conflict. Sometimes parents urge their children to divorce their partners as a way to deal with **rifts**.

10 Women are more likely to be the ones who suffer financially when this happens. Rising divorce rates reflect the spread of more tolerant, permissive values towards women, but legislation tends to favor men in divorce settlements. A legal interpretation issued in 2003 says that if a divorce is disputed, property bought for one partner by a spouse's parents before marriage can revert to the partner alone. That usually means the husband's family: they often try to increase their child's ability to attract a mate by buying him a home.

11 In 2011, the Supreme Court went further. It ruled that in contested cases (as about one-fifth of divorces are), the property would be considered that of one partner alone if that partner's parents had bought it for him or her after the couple had got married. In addition, if one partner (rather than his or her parents) had bought a home before the couple wed, that person could be awarded sole ownership by a divorce court. This ruling has put women at a disadvantage too: by convention they are less often named on deeds.

12 In practice, if the couple has children, the person with custody often keeps the home—more often the mother. Yet the court's interpretation sets a worrying precedent for divorced women. Their difficulties may be

compounded by the two-child policy, which came into effect on January 1st. If couples have two children and both partners want custody, judges often assign parents one child each. Marriage and the family are still strong in China—but children clearly lie in a different asset class.

Words and Phrases

buck	/bʌk/	*v.*	to oppose something in a direct way 抵制；反对
		e.g.	The mayor bucked at the school board's suggestion.
celebratory	/ˌseləˈbreɪtəri/	*adj.*	done in order to celebrate a particular event or occasion 庆祝的；祝贺的
		e.g.	When we heard she'd got the job, we all went off for a celebratory drink.
compound	/kɒmˈpaʊnd/	*v.*	to make a difficult situation worse by adding more problems 使加剧，恶化
		e.g.	His financial problems were compounded when he unexpectedly lost his job.
conjugal	/ˈkɒndʒəgəl/	*adj.*	relating to marriage 婚姻的，夫妻之间的
		e.g.	A couple's conjugal fate is prearranged.
contemplate	/ˈkɒntəmpleɪt/	*v.*	to think about something seriously for a period of time 考虑，思量
		e.g.	For a time he contemplated a career as an army medical doctor.
cramped	/kræmpt/	*adj.*	unable to move properly and feeling uncomfortable because there is not enough space 拥挤的，狭小的
		e.g.	There are hundreds of families living in cramped conditions on the floor of the airport lounge.
dissolve	/dɪˈzɒlv/	*v.*	to formally end a parliament, business arrangement, marriage, etc. 解散；终止
		e.g.	Parliament has been dissolved.
fret	/fret/	*v.*	to worry about something, especially when there is no need（使）烦恼，（使）焦急
		e.g.	I sit in meetings, fretting about what was happening at home.
fuel	/ˈfjuːəl/	*v.*	to make something, especially something bad, increase or become stronger 使恶化；使更强烈

			e.g. The rapid promotion of the director's son has itself fuelled resentment within the company.
luster	/ˈlʌstə/	n.	the quality that makes something interesting or exciting 光彩，光辉
			e.g. A good name keeps its luster in the dark.
pool	/puːl/	v.	to combine your money, ideas, skills, etc. with those of other people so that you can all use them 集合（资金/资源）
			e.g. The kids pooled their money to buy their parents a wedding anniversary gift.
rift	/rɪft/	n.	a situation in which two people or groups have had a serious disagreement and begun to dislike and not trust each other（人际关系的）裂痕；分歧，不和
			e.g. The marriage caused a rift between the brothers and they didn't speak to each other for ten years.
soar	/sɔː/	v.	to increase quickly to a high level 上升，增加
			e.g. The price of petrol has soared in recent weeks.

Reading Comprehension

Task 1 Text A can be divided into the following four sections. Read the text carefully and work in pairs to find the main idea of each section. Then complete the following table.

Introduction (Para. 1)	• Yang Yourong's wife kicks him as they walk upstairs and follows again to the _____ offices of a district-government bureau handling _____ in Chongqing.
Changes relating to divorce rates (Paras. 2–6)	• This is a remarkable transformation in a society where for centuries marriage was _____. • Social and economic changes: 1) In the past 35 years, _____ has been tearing families apart. 2) _____ have been giving way to more liberal ones. 3) Women are becoming _____, and more aware of their _____. 4) Greater affluence has made it easier for many people to _____.

Unit 4 Society

Reasons for rising divorce rates (Paras. 7–9)	• It is _____ that is partly to blame for rising divorce rates. Conservative attitudes to _____ _____ result in Chinese youths having fewer of them than their counterparts in the West. • _____ are part of the problem too. _____ is becoming more common.
Women suffer financially in divorce (Paras. 10–12)	• Rising divorce rates reflect the spread of _____ towards women, but legislation tends to _____ in divorce settlements.

Task 2 Based on the information in Task 1, write a summary of the text in 80–100 words. Try to make your paragraph logical and coherent.

Task 3 Work in groups to discuss the following questions.

1. What are the traditional Chinese values on marriage?
2. What are the reasons for the rising divorce rates?
3. What changes have taken place along with the rising divorce rates?
4. How do you think about the current legislation on divorce?
5. Some people say the improvement of women's condition leads to the rising divorce rates. What do you think of it? Explain your idea.

Vocabulary

Task 1 For each sentence there are four choices marked A, B, C, and D. Choose the one that best keeps the meaning with the underlined part.

1. In later years he lived in a rather cramped little flat in Bristol.

    A. defined   B. confirmed   C. confined   D. contained

2. TPG bought the firm as a joint venture with an entrepreneur in 2006 just as the demand for cars began to soar in China.

    A. increase   B. swing   C. stop   D. decrease

3. If you want some time alone to contemplate your options now, clearly let others know that you need a bit of space.

   A. contempt   B. consider   C. conclude   D. conceive

4. He has warned that the serious rifts within the country could lead to civil war.

   A. disappointments B. disengagements   C. dismiss   D. disagreements

5. The main thing to do is to always go with the trend and never buck the trend, regardless of how much capital you have.

   A. resist   B. reboot   C. rebate   D. revive

6. He said the government should consider lowering the standard in deciding whether to initiate disputes.

   A. implement   B. begin   C. invent   D. involve

7. We were all given by magic the power to read each other's thoughts, I suppose the first effect would be to dissolve all friendships.

   A. solve   B. dismiss   C. dismember   D. end

8. In the policy level, the current implementation of the subsidy policy in the industry seems to be in dispute.

   A. disability   B. disadvantage   C. disagreement   D. discussion

9. When you're in a bad mood, it's easy to look for things to fuel that bad mood or reinforce it.

   A. reduce   B. increase   C. cause   D. burn

10. His financial problems were compounded when he unexpectedly lost his job.

    A. complicated   B. composed   C. completed   D. aggravated

Task 2   Complete the following sentences with the words and phrases given below. Change the form if necessary.

renewal	celebratory	retain	pool
fret	reckon	watch over	tear apart
split up	fall out of love		

1. It's the little things that _____ even the most solid marriages.
2. She's always _____ about the children.
3. The robbers _____ the house to look for the money.
4. You have the right to _____ possession of the goods.
5. Steve's parents _____ when he was four.
6. Investors agreed to _____ their resources to develop the property.
7. The _____ event will mark the 75th anniversary of the university.
8. It was a week-long festival celebrating the _____ of the city and its continued prosperity.
9. The prince has two bodyguards _____ him every hour of the day.
10. The police _____ that whoever killed Dad was with him earlier that day.

Translation

Task 1   Translate the following paragraph into Chinese.

   The trend reflects profound economic and social change. In the past 35 years, the biggest internal migration experienced by any country in human history has been tearing families apart. Traditional values have been giving way to more liberal ones. Women are becoming better educated, and more aware of their marital rights (they now initiate over half of all divorce cases). Greater affluence has made it easier for many people to contemplate living alone—no longer is there such an incentive to stay married in order to pool resources.

Task 2　Translate the following paragraph into English with the help of the words in brackets.

20世纪80年代以来，中国社会发生了巨大的变革，人们对待婚姻家庭的态度也随之改变，传统的婚姻观念让位给现在多样化的形态。现代人认为离婚是一种生活状态的改变，是寻找新幸福的出口。个人价值的凸显、女性经济和社会地位的独立以及物质生活的富裕都与离婚率的急剧增长密不可分。正如媒体所言，离婚对于社会的稳定以及犯罪都是一大威胁。离婚时女性更容易遭受经济重创，除双方物质财产外，孩子的监护权也成为争夺的焦点。（give way to, soar, reckon, custody）

Growing Grey
Read **Text B** online and do the exercises.

Unit 4　Society

Writing Focus

Problem-solution Essay

Introduction

Problem-solution essay is a very common type of academic essay. Its purpose is to explain in details the nature of the problem, and provide effective solutions to the problem. This type of essay is very useful in academic studies because it helps readers understand the problem thoroughly by analyzing and working out possible solutions.

Exercise 1　Have you written a problem-solution essay before? What's the topic? What solutions did you propose? And were they effective?

_____

_____

Features of a Problem-solution Essay

A proper problem-solution essay usually includes a clear thesis statement, convincing details that support your statement, and transitional signals that connect the sentences smoothly.

Thesis statement	Both the problem and solution should be included in the thesis statement.
Supporting details	Anecdotes, examples, facts or statistics are supposed to be used to argue advantages and disadvantages, as well as the feasibility of the proposed solutions.

Transitional signals	Signals that indicate the cause of a problem, such as *because, as, since, due to, owing to, because of, thanks to…* Signals that indicate the result of a problem, such as *hence, thus, therefore, as a consequence, accordingly, as a result, consequently, so… that…* Signals that indicate different solutions, such as *first, second, last…*

Exercise 2 Read the essay below and answer the following questions.

Writer's Block

You have to finish that report for the boss, write an essay or article, or you work in the information economy—the deadline for the current project is looming but you find yourself mindlessly staring at a blank page on the screen and the words just won't come.

Writers' block is not an uncommon experience. The root cause is anxiety. There are many reasons for the writer to feel anxious. Perfectionism is one of them—the writer is too judgemental, viewing her work as inferior in some way. The project itself may be fundamentally misconceived or the writer lacks the experience or ability to complete it. Perhaps the pressure of a tight deadline is paralysing. There are other anxiety-provoking life stresses and deep-seated issues: serious illness, depression, a relationship break-up, not to mention financial difficulties. Sometimes distractions are too great or the writer simply runs out of inspiration.

There are various ways of overcoming the block. First, exercise gets the blood moving through the body and brain: a visit to the gym, a walk around the block, a few yoga poses and some deep breathing all help to clear the head, induce relaxation and get the creative juices flowing. Then, the body and brain need to be nourished with healthy food and pure water. Junk food is unlikely to increase mental output. Finally, distractions have to be completely eliminated—phones turned off, the Internet disconnected, the desk or workspace uncluttered—because good writing needs focus and undivided attention.

1. Does this essay have a thesis statement? If not, write one.

_____

_____

2. How many solutions are provided in this essay? Can you identify them quickly? And why?

_____

_____

3. Do you think these solutions are well argued? Why or why not?

_____

_____

Format of a Problem-solution Essay

The problem-solution essay has two main formats: the block-structure format and the chain-structure format.

Block-structure format		Chain-structure format
Introduction	Introduction	Introduction
Body	Body	Body
Solution 1	Problem 1	Problem 1
Solution 2	Problem 2	Solution to problem 1
Solution 3	Problem 3	Problem 2
Conclusion	Solution 1	Solution to problem 2
	Solution 2	Problem 3
	Solution 3	Solution to problem 3
	Conclusion	Conclusion

There are two types of the block-structure, and the differences lie in the introduction and body. In the first type, the introduction part includes the present situation and the analysis of the problem, and the body part is composed of all the solutions. In the second type, the present situation is presented in the introduction part. In the body part, all the problems (or just one problem) are listed at the beginning, and then all the solutions are listed afterwards. The conclusion part of these two types are arranged in the same way, which may include a brief summary and an evaluation of the solutions.

For the chain-structure format, the introduction and conclusion part are arranged in the same way as the second type of block structure. The only difference lies in the body part: each problem is followed

immediately by the solutions to this specific problem.

Both formats are effective and you can choose the most suitable one for your essay. For example, if there's only one problem discussed in the article, you may have to choose the block structure. If there are several problems discussed, then you can choose either one. Often, the block structure is more suitable for short essays for its structure is clearer and simpler.

Exercise 3 Read the essay below and answer the following questions.

Obesity and Poor Fitness

Consumption of processed and convenience foods and our dependence on the car have led to an increase in obesity and reduction in the fitness level of the adult population. In some countries, especially industrialized ones, the number of obese people can amount to one third of the population. This is significant as obesity and poor fitness lead to a decrease in life expectancy, and it is therefore important for individuals and governments to work together to tackle this issue and improve their citizens' diet and fitness.

Obesity and poor fitness decrease life expectancy. Overweight people are more likely to have serious illnesses such as diabetes and heart disease, which can result in premature death. It is well known that regular exercise can reduce the risk of heart disease and stroke, which means that those with poor fitness levels are at an increased risk of suffering from those problems.

Changes by individuals to their diet and their physical activity can increase life expectancy. There is a reliance today on the consumption of processed foods, which have a high fat and sugar content. By preparing their own foods, and consuming more fruit and vegetables, people could ensure that their diets are healthier and more balanced, which could lead to a reduction in obesity levels. In order to improve fitness levels, people could choose to walk or cycle to work or to the shops rather than taking the car. They could also choose to walk upstairs instead of taking the lift. These simple changes could lead to a significant improvement in fitness levels.

Governments could also implement initiatives to improve their citizens' eating and exercise habits. This could be done through education, for example by adding classes to the curriculum about healthy diet and lifestyles. Governments could also do more to encourage their citizens to walk or cycle instead of taking the car, for instance by building more cycle lanes or increasing vehicle taxes. While some might argue that increased taxes are a negative way to solve the problem, it is no different from the high taxes imposed on cigarettes to reduce cigarette consumption.

In short, obesity and poor fitness are a significant problem in modern life, leading to lower life expectancy. Individuals and governments can work together to tackle this problem and so improve diet and fitness. Of the solutions suggested, those made by individuals themselves are likely to have more impact, though it is clear that a concerted effort with the government is essential for success. With obesity levels in industrialized and industrializing countries continuing to rise, it is essential that we take actions now to deal with this problem.

1. Which structure is used in this essay? Why does the author choose this structure?

2. Which sentence is the thesis statement of this essay? Do you think it is a good one?

3. How many solutions are proposed in this essay? Do they support the thesis statement well?

4. How does the author end the essay?

Sample Essay Analysis

Crop-growing Skyscrapers

By the year 2050, nearly 80% of the Earth's population will live in urban centres. Applying the most conservative estimates to current demographic trends, the human population will increase by about three billion people by then. An estimated 109 hectares of new land (about 20% larger than Brazil) will be needed to grow enough food to feed them, if traditional farming methods continue as they are practiced today. At present, throughout the world, over 80% of the land that is suitable for raising crops is in use. Historically, some 15% of that has been laid waste by poor management practices. What can be done to ensure enough food for the world's population to live on? The answer is indoor farming. Many believe an entirely new approach to indoor farming is required to accommodate another three billion people, employing cutting-edge technologies.

One such proposal is for the "Vertical Farm". The concept is of multi-storey buildings in which food crops are grown in environmentally controlled conditions. Situated in the heart of urban centres, they would drastically reduce the amount of transportation required to bring food to consumers. Vertical farms would need to be efficient, cheap to construct and safe to operate. If successfully implemented, proponents claim, vertical farms offer the promise of urban renewal, sustainable production of a safe and varied food supply (through year-round production of all crops), and the eventual repair of ecosystems that have been sacrificed for horizontal farming.

The supporters of vertical farming claim many potential advantages for the system. For instance, crops would be produced all year round, as they would be kept in artificially controlled, optimum growing conditions. There would be no weather-related crop failures due to droughts, floods or pests. All the food could be grown organically, eliminating the need for herbicides, pesticides and fertilizers. The system would greatly reduce the incidence of many infectious diseases that are acquired at the agricultural interface. Although the system would consume energy, it would return energy to the grid via methane generation from composting non-edible parts of plants. It would also dramatically reduce fossil fuel use, by cutting out the need for tractors, ploughs and shipping.

A major drawback of vertical farming, however, is that the plants would require artificial light. Without it, those plants nearest the windows would be exposed to more sunlight and grow more quickly, reducing the efficiency of the system. Single-storey greenhouses have the benefit of natural overhead light: even so, many still need artificial lighting. A multi-storey facility with no natural overhead light would require far more. Generating enough light could be prohibitively expensive, unless cheap, renewable energy is available, and this appears to be rather a future aspiration than a likelihood for the near future.

One variation on vertical farming that has been developed is to grow plants in stacked trays that move on rails. Moving the trays allows the plants to get enough sunlight. This system is already in operation, and works well within a single-storey greenhouse with light reaching it from above: it is not certain, however, that it can be made to work without that overhead natural light.

Vertical farming is an attempt to address the undoubted problems that we face in producing enough food for a growing population. At the moment, though, more needs to be done to reduce the detrimental impact it would have on the environment, particularly as regards the use of energy. While it is possible that much of our food will be grown in skyscrapers in the future, most experts currently believe it is far more likely that we will simply use the space available on urban rooftops.

Exercise 4   Read the essay above and answer the following questions.

1. What is the problem discussed in this essay? Does the author clearly present the causes and effects of the problem? Are you convinced that the problem is important and needs to be solved?

   _____

   _____

2. Which sentence is the thesis statement of this essay? Is it a good one?

   _____

   _____

3. This essay uses the first type of the block-structure format, but the body part (Paras 2–5) is too long. Summarize the body paragraphs into one paragraph.

   _____

   _____

4. Which statement best describes the conclusion paragraph of this essay?

  A. It ends with the prediction of how the situation will change if the solution is adopted.

  B. It makes a recommendation.

  C. It combines a summary with the evaluation of the solution and a prediction.

  D. It reemphasizes the importance of the problem.

Writing Practice

Task Read the short introduction below. Develop this introduction into a problem-solution essay using the techniques you have learned in this unit.

Bullying in the Workplace

When workmates use offensive or intimidating behavior to humiliate other workers, it is a form of abuse. Bullies are frequently insecure people with low self-esteem (although it may not be obvious). Their targets are usually competent, honest, and independent people who get on well with their colleagues—often the very characteristic which bullies feel they lack. Bullies are often most concerned with gaining power and exerting dominance over people by causing fear and distress.

UNIT 5
Education

Introduction

It is estimated that 60%–75% of the world's population is bilingual, and bilingual education has long been a common educational method used all over the world. A number of studies provide evidence for the effectiveness of bilingual education. Suggestopedia, which emphasizes use of positive suggestion, is another teaching approach used mostly in foreign language learning context. What do you think are the benefits of bilingual education? How can suggestopedia be helpful to promote language learning? In this unit, you'll read two texts which might help you get some information about the two questions.

Learning Objectives

Reading

- Understanding the benefits of bilingual education
- Recognizing the power of positive suggestion from a book review
- Identifying the essay structure of an educational study
- Talking about bilingual education and language teaching methods

Writing

- Identifying the features of a cause and effect essay
- Analyzing the format of a cause and effect essay
- Learning different patterns of organizing supporting paragraphs
- Writing a cause and effect essay

Unit 5　**Education**

Text A

🎓 Topic Exploration

Step 1 Use a library catalogue or Internet sources to search for relevant books or articles about *Bilingual Education*. Share your readings with your group members.

Step 2 Work in groups to prepare a presentation of the books or articles you previously read. Be sure to include:
- the definition of bilingual education
- two studies about bilingual education
- the similarities and differences on the findings or views of the studies you read

Step 3 Report your work to the whole class.

🎓 Reading

The Benefits of Being Bilingual[1]

1　According to the latest figures, the majority of the world's population is now bilingual or **multilingual**, having grown up speaking two or more languages. In the past, such children were considered to be at a disadvantage compared with their monolingual peers. Over the past few

---

1　This text is adapted from "The Cognitive Benefits of Being Bilingual" by Marian, V., & Shook, A. (2012). *Cerebrum: The Dana Forum on Brain Science*, October 31st.

decades, however, technological advances have allowed researchers to look more deeply at how bilingualism interacts with and changes the **cognitive** and **neurological** systems, thereby identifying several clear benefits of being bilingual.

2   Research shows that when a bilingual person uses one language, the other is active at the same time. When we hear a word, we don't hear the entire word all at once: the sounds arrive in **sequential** order. Long before the word is finished, the brain's language system begins to guess what that word might be. If you hear "can", you will likely **activate** words like "candy" and "candle" as well, at least during the earlier stages of word recognition. For bilingual people, this activation is not limited to a single language; **auditory** input activates corresponding words regardless of the language to which they belong. Some of the most **compelling** evidence for this phenomenon, called "language co-activation"[2], comes from studying eye movements. A Russian-English bilingual asked to "pick up a marker" from a set of objects would look more at a stamp than someone who doesn't know Russian, because the Russian word for "stamp", marka, sounds like the English word he or she heard, "marker". In cases like this, language co-activation occurs because what the listener hears could map onto words in either language.

3   Having to deal with this persistent linguistic competition can result in difficulties, however. For instance, knowing more than one language can cause speakers to name pictures more slowly, and can increase "tip-of-the-tongue states"[3], when you can almost, but not quite, bring a word to mind. As a result, the constant **juggling** of two languages creates a need to control how much a person accesses a language at any given time. For this reason, bilingual people often perform better on tasks that require conflict management. In the classic Stroop Task, people see a word and are asked to name the color of the word's font. When the color and the word match (i.e. the word "red" printed in red), people correctly name the color more

---

2   language co-activation: the process of engaging both languages simultaneously by bilingual people.

3   tip-of-the-tongue states: This phenomenon is the subjective feeling that people have of being confident that they know the target word for which they are searching, yet they cannot recall this word.

quickly than when the color and the word don't match (i.e. the word "red" printed in blue). This occurs because the word itself ("red") and its font color (blue) conflict. Bilingual people often **excel at** tasks such as this, which tap into the ability to ignore competing **perceptual** information and focus on the relevant aspects of the input. Bilinguals are also better at switching between two tasks; for example, when bilinguals have to switch from categorizing objects by color (red or green) to categorizing them by shape (circle or triangle), they do so more quickly than monolingual people, reflecting better cognitive control when having to make rapid changes of strategy.

4   It also seems that the neurological roots of the bilingual advantage extend to brain areas more traditionally associated with sensory processing. When **monolingual** and bilingual **adolescents** listen to simple speech sounds without any **intervening** background noise, they show highly similar brain stem responses. When researchers play the same sound to both groups in the presence of background noise, however, the bilingual listeners' neural response is considerably larger, reflecting better **encoding** of the sound's fundamental frequency, a feature of sound closely related to **pitch** perception.

5   Such improvements in cognitive and sensory processing may help a bilingual person to process information in the environment, and help explain why bilingual adults **acquire** a third language better than monolingual adults master a second language. This advantage may be rooted in the skill of focusing on information about the new language while reducing interference from the languages they already know.

6   Research also indicates that bilingual experience may help to **keep** the cognitive mechanisms **sharp** by **recruiting alternate** brain networks to compensate for those that become damaged during aging. Older bilinguals enjoy improved memory **relative to** monolingual people, which can lead to real-world health benefits. In a study of over 200 patients with Alzheimer's disease[4], a **degenerative** brain disease,

---

4   Alzheimer's disease: a progressive disease that destroys memory and other important mental functions. At first, someone with Alzheimer's disease may notice mild confusion and difficulty remembering. Eventually, people with the disease may even forget important people in their lives and undergo dramatic personality changes.

bilingual patients reported showing initial symptoms of the disease an average of five years later than monolingual patients. In a follow-up study, researchers compared the brains of bilingual and monolingual patients matched on the **severity** of Alzheimer's symptoms. Surprisingly, the bilinguals' brains had more physical signs of disease than their monolingual **counterparts**, even though their outward behavior and abilities were similar. If the brain is an engine, bilingualism may help it to go farther on the same amount of fuel.

7   Furthermore, the benefits associated with bilingual experience seem to start very early. In one study, researchers taught seven-month-old babies growing up in monolingual or bilingual homes that when they heard a tinkling sound, a puppet appeared on one side of a screen. Halfway through the study, the puppet began appearing on the opposite side of the screen. In order to get a reward, the infants had to adjust the rule they'd learned; only the bilingual babies were able to successfully learn the new rule. This suggests that for very young children, as well as for older people, **navigating** a multilingual environment imparts advantages that transfer far beyond language.

Words and Phrases

acquire	/ə'kwaɪə/	v.	to gain knowledge or learn a skill 习得；学到；获得
		e.g.	She has acquired a good knowledge of English.
activate	/'æktɪveɪt/	v.	to make an electrical system or chemical process start working 激活；启动，开动
		e.g.	The gene is activated by a specific protein.
adolescent	/ˌædə'lesənt/	n.	a young person, usually between the ages of 12 and 18, who is developing into an adult 青少年
		e.g.	John changed from a friendly and cheerful young boy into a confused adolescent.
alternate	/ɔːl'tɜːnət/	adj.	(of two things) happening or following one after the other regularly（两事物）交替的；间隔的
		e.g.	John has to work on alternate Sundays.
auditory	/'ɔːdətəri/	adj.	relating to the ability to hear 听的，听觉的

Unit 5 Education

		e.g. A growing body of evidence points to the importance of early auditory input for developing language skills.
cognitive	/ˈkɒɡnətɪv/	*adj.* related to the process of knowing, understanding, and learning something 认知的；感知的
		e.g. As children grow older, their cognitive processes become sharper.
compelling	/kəmˈpelɪŋ/	*adj.* (of an argument, evidence, etc.) convincing 令人信服的，很有说服力的
		e.g. It's a fairly compelling argument for going into town.
counterpart	/ˈkaʊntəpɑːt/	*n.* someone or something that has the same job or purpose as someone or something else in a different place 职位（作用）相当的人；相对应的事物
		e.g. The prime minister is to meet his European counterparts to discuss the war against drugs.
degenerative	/dɪˈdʒenərətɪv/	*adj.* (of an illness) getting or likely to get worse as time passes（疾病）恶化的，变性的；退化的
		e.g. All these are degenerative diseases of the central nervous system.
encode	/ɪnˈkəʊd/	*v.* to put a message or other information into code 把……编码
		e.g. Some music CDs are encoded with information about the performers and their music.
excel at		to do something very well, or much better than most people 擅长；善于
		e.g. She has always excelled at foreign languages.
intervening	/ˌɪntəˈviːnɪŋ/	*adj.* coming or existing between two events, dates, objects, etc. 发生于其间的；介于中间的
		e.g. Little had changed in the intervening years.
juggling	/ˈdʒʌɡəlɪŋ/	*n.* the practice of changing things or arranging them in a way that makes it possible for you to do something 重新安排；尽量兼顾
		e.g. It took a lot of juggling and rearrangement of figures before the loan was approved.
keep... sharp		keep alert, be cautious 保持敏锐、警惕的状态
		e.g. This is a very important game. I want everyone to keep sharp the whole time.
monolingual	/ˌmɒnəʊˈlɪŋɡwəl/	*adj.* speaking or using only one language 单语的
		e.g. This is a monolingual dictionary.

multilingual	/ˌmʌltɪˈlɪŋgwəl/	*adj.*	using, speaking, or written in several different languages 多种语言的
		e.g.	It offers multilingual and interdisciplinary curriculum at university degree level.
navigate	/ˈnævɪgeɪt/	*v.*	to understand or deal with something complicated 驾驭；成功应付（困难处境）
		e.g.	This outlook helped her to navigate through her later years with success.
neurological	/ˌnjʊərəˈlɒdʒɪkəl/	*adj.*	relating to nerves or to the science of neurology 神经（病）学的
		e.g.	Alzheimer's disease is a neurological disorder.
perceptual	/pərˈseptʃuəl/	*adj.*	relating to the ability to perceive things or the process of perceiving 知觉的；感知的
		e.g.	It also showed that mere exposure to the perceptual stimuli used during practice on these tasks does not generate learning.
pitch	/pɪtʃ/	*n.*	how high or low a note or other sound is （尤指乐音的）音高
		e.g.	Ultrasonic waves are at a higher pitch than the human ear can hear.
recruit	/rɪˈkruːt/	*v.*	to find new people to work in a company, join an organization, do a job, etc. 吸收（新成员）；征募（新兵）
		e.g.	If there are proper projects for us to participate in, we will recruit more volunteers and staff.
relative to			with regard to; in connection with 相对于；涉及
		e.g.	Employment in primary and secondary industries has declined relative to population.
sequential	/sɪˈkwenʃəl/	*adj.*	following in order of time or place 顺序的；连续的
		e.g.	Some industry figures have indicated that high sequential sales gains may not be sustainable.
severity	/səˈverəti/	*n.*	the fact or condition of something being extremely bad or serious 严重；严格
		e.g.	Several drugs are used to lessen the severity of the symptoms.

Unit 5 Education

Reading Comprehension

Task 1 Text A can be divided into the following two sections. Read the text carefully and work in pairs to find the main idea of each section. Then complete the following table.

Introduction (Para. 1)	• Attitudes towards bilingualism have changed in recent years. 1) In the past, bilingual children were considered to be _____ _____ compared with their monolingual peers. 2) Over the past few decades, researchers examined how bilingualism interacts with and changes the _____ and _____ systems, thereby identifying several clear benefits of _____.
Research findings (Paras. 2–7)	• Test 1: Observing the _____ of Russian-English bilingual people when asked to select certain objects. Findings: Bilingual people engage both languages simultaneously, and this mechanism is known as _____. • Test 2: A test called the _____, focusing on naming colours. Findings: Bilingual people are more able to handle tasks involving a skill called _____. • Test 3: A test involving switching between tasks. Findings: When changing strategies, bilingual people have superior _____.
	• Test 4: Playing the same sound to both bilingual and monolingual groups in the presence of _____. Findings: Bilingual listeners showed larger _____ _____, which indicates that bilingual people have better _____. • Test 5: A study of over 200 patients with _____. Findings: Bilingual patients reported showing initial symptoms of the disease an average of _____ later than monolingual counterparts. • Test 6: A study of seven-month-old babies responding to the change of the position of puppets on the screen. Findings: A bilingual baby could adjust the rule they have learned and successfully _____.

Task 2 Based on the information in Task 1, write a summary of the text in 80–100 words. Try to make your paragraph logical and coherent.

Task 3 Work in groups to discuss the following questions.

1. What are people's attitudes towards bilingualism in recent years?

2. What are the advantages of being bilingual according to the author?

3. Are there any negative consequences of bilingualism? What are they?

4. How do you understand the sentence "If the brain is an engine, bilingualism may help it to go farther on the same amount of fuel."?

5. What is your attitude towards bilingual education?

Vocabulary

Task 1 For each sentence there are four choices marked A, B, C, and D. Choose the one that best keeps the meaning with the underlined part.

1. If you manage to <u>navigate</u> a difficult situation, you will accomplish it successfully.

    A. handle   B. steer   C. guide   D. locate

2. Previously it had only been known that highly trained musicians have highly developed <u>auditory</u> abilities compared to non-musicians.

    A. expressive   B. hearing   C. oral   D. visual

3. All employers should give respect to employees' personal information files while trying to <u>recruit</u> people.

    A. judge   B. discover   C. employ   D. reject

4. The alarm is <u>activated</u> by the lightest pressure.

    A. adjusted   B. triggered   C. caused   D. monitored

Unit 5 **Education**

5. I feel that my enthusiasm, diligence, ad adaptability could <u>compensate for</u> the lack of experience.

  A. apply for   B. make up for   C. allow for   D. account for

6. The new studies provide <u>compelling</u> evidence in support of these concepts.

  A. convincing   B. enforcing   C. adequate   D. conclusive

7. Participants were <u>categorized</u> according to age.

  A. identified   B. classified   C. specified   D. verified

8. What would you do differently if you had the time and energy to <u>tap into</u> your creativity?

  A. discover   B. develop   C. identify   D. specify

9. It will take three months to <u>acquire</u> the necessary skills.

  A. gain   B. require   C. fulfill   D. achieve

10. We can never eliminate financial crises, but we can reduce their likelihood and <u>severity</u>.

  A. security   B. seriousness   C. sensitivity   D. scarcity

Task 2 *Complete the following sentences with the words and phrases given below. Change the form if necessary.*

activate	alternate	bilingual	mechanism
counterpart	perceptual	excel in	sequential
relative to	keep… sharp		

1. The Foreign Minister held talks with his Chinese _____.

2. International travel has grown to the point that many hotels find it necessary to employ _____ or even multilingual staff members.

3. This is called the _____ stage of cognition, namely, the stage of sense perceptions and impressions.

4. There's no _____ for punishing arms exporters who break the rules.

5. It has been a week of _____ sunshine and rain.

6. We have sent you an email with a(n) _____ link for you to confirm your email address.

7. The buying process is analyzed as a series of _____ steps.

8. House prices now look cheap _____ earnings.

9. Mounting evidence suggests that regular exercise can _____ your mind _____ and increase learning and memory capacity.

10. Florida is not normally considered to be a major manufacturing state, yet it does _____ some areas, such as medical device manufacturing.

Translation

Task 1 Translate the following paragraph into Chinese.

Research also indicates that bilingual experience may help to keep the cognitive mechanisms sharp by recruiting alternate brain networks to compensate for those that become damaged during aging. Older bilinguals enjoy improved memory relative to monolingual people, which can lead to real-world health benefits. In a study of over 200 patients with Alzheimer's disease, a degenerative brain disease, bilingual patients reported showing initial symptoms of the disease an average of five years later than monolingual patients.

Task 2 Translate the following paragraph into English with the help of the words in brackets.

学习第二语言的过程可以抑制与年龄相关的恶化的疾病。与单语者相比，双语者在生命早期患上老年痴呆和阿尔茨海默氏症的可能性更小。掌握第二语言的人的压力水平会更低，神经健康状况会更好。此外，双语者倾向于拥有更好的认知技能。在学校，会说另一种语言的学生在学术考试中表现更好。他们的大脑能够保持活跃、警觉和敏锐，因此在处理不同的任务时能够达到平衡。（bilingual, neurological, cognitive, excel in）

Text B **Educating Psyche**

Read **Text B** online and do the exercises.

Cause and Effect Essay

Introduction

Why has the haze in China become serious in recent years? How will the world be changed by artificial intelligence? What are the causes of cyber bullying? These are some common topics in academic study, and when looking for the answers to these questions, we are ready to write a cause and effect essay.

The main purpose of a cause and effect essay is to explain the causes of a natural or social phenomenon, or the effects of a phenomenon, or a combination of both. For instance, if your purpose is to show the impact of energy shortage, your essay will focus on its effects. If your purpose is to explain why online shopping is so popular, your essay will focus on the causes. If your purpose is to discuss the reasons for global warming and its influences, your essay will focus on both causes and effects.

Exercise 1 Discuss with your partner and list some cause and effect essay topics related to your major. The first three are examples.

- Effects of death penalties on crime (if your major is law).
- What caused the recent stock market slump or soar in China (if your major is finance)?
- What is the impact of cancer research on reducing cancer mortality (if your major is medicine)?
- _____
- _____

Features of a Cause and Effect Essay

Below are features of a cause and effect essay.

Thesis statement	Present the purpose (cause or effect or a combination of both) of the essay.
Patterns of organization	The supporting paragraphs should be arranged in climactic order (order of importance).
Transitional signals	Signals that indicate the cause, such as *because, as, since, due to, owing to, because of, thanks to*, etc. Signals that indicate the effect, such as *hence, thus, therefore, as a consequence, accordingly, as a result, consequently, so... that...*, etc.

Exercise 2 Read the outline below and answer the questions about the features of a cause and effect essay.

All the main languages have been studied prescriptively, especially in the 18th century approach to the writing of grammars and dictionaries. The aims of these early grammarians were threefold.

First, they wanted to codify the principles of their languages, to show that there was a system beneath the apparent chaos of usage.

Second, they wanted a means of settling disputes over usage.

Finally, they wanted to point out what they felt to be common errors, in order to "improve" the language.

1. Does the thesis statement indicate the author's purpose?

_____

_____

2. Which organizational pattern is used in the outline to arrange the supporting paragraphs?

_____

_____

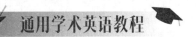

Format of a Cause and Effect Essay

There are generally three types of formats of a cause and effect essay depending on writer's purposes:

Cause essay	Effect essay	Cause and effect essay

Introduction
Main body
    Cause 1
    Cause 2
    Cause 3
Conclusion
	Introduction
	Main body
	    Effect 1
	    Effect 2
	    Effect 3
	Conclusion
		Introduction
		Main body
		    Cause 1
		    Cause 2
		    Effect 1
		    Effect 2
		Conclusion

No matter which format you choose, there are some basic principles that need to be followed. First, the last sentence of the introduction should be the thesis statement. Second, each supporting paragraph in the main body should have a topic sentence. Third, do not add new information in the conclusion. After you finish the first draft, you need to revise the essay from the aspects of unity, support, coherence, and sentence skills. To achieve unity means that all the evidence and supporting details are closely related to the thesis statement and the topic sentences. Good supporting details should be vivid and specific. Another aspect to consider is coherence, and there are three techniques to achieve coherence: transitional signals, lexical devices, and logical order.

Exercise 3 Read the following topics and write an outline based on the three formats listed above. The first is an example.

1. What causes the writer's block?

   Cause essay format:

   Thesis statement: The root cause for writer's block is anxiety, and there are several reasons for the writer to feel anxious.

   Cause 1: Perfectionism is one of them—the writer is too judgmental, viewing the work as inferior in some way.

   Cause 2: The project itself may be fundamentally misconceived or the writer lacks the experience or ability to complete it.

Unit 5   **Education**

   Cause 3: The pressure of a tight deadline is paralyzing.

2. What causes parents to over-schedule their children's activities?
   Cause essay format:
   Thesis statement: _____
   Cause 1: _____
   Cause 2: _____
   Cause 3: _____

3. What effects has social media had on family relationships?
   Effect essay format:
   Thesis statement: _____
   Effect 1: _____
   Effect 2: _____

4. What are the causes of men still out-earning women in wages? What are the effects?
   Cause and effect essay format:
   Thesis statement: _____
   Cause 1: _____
   Cause 2: _____
   Effect 1: _____
   Effect 2: _____

Sample Essay Analysis

Taming the Anger Monster

1   No one would deny that we are one angry society. An entire vocabulary has grown up to describe situations of out-of-control fury: road rage, sideline rage, computer rage, biker rage, air rage. Bookstore shelves are filled with authors' advice on how to deal with our anger. What has happened to us? Are we that much angrier than we used to be? Have we lost all inhibitions about expressing our anger? Are we, as a society, literally losing our ability to control our tempers? There are three components to blame for our societal bad behavior: time, technology and tension.

2   To begin with, what's eating up our time? Americans work longer hours and are rewarded with less vacation time than people in any other industrial society. Over an average year, for example, most British employees work 250 hours less than most Americans. Most Germans work a full 500 hours less. And most Europeans are given four to six weeks' vacation every year compared to the average American's two weeks. To make matters worse, many Americans face long stressful commutes at the beginning and end of each long workday.

3   Once we Americans finally get home from work, our busy day is rarely done. We are involved in community activities; our children participate in sports, school programs, and extra-curricular activities; and our houses, yards and cars cry out for maintenance. To make matters worse, we are reluctant to use the little bit of leisure time we do have to catch up on our sleep. Compared with Americans of the nineteenth and early twentieth century, most of us are chronically sleep-deprived. While our ancestors typically slept nine-and-a-half hours a night, many of us feel lucky to get seven.

4   The bottom line: We are time-challenged and just plain tired—and tired people are cranky people. We're ready to blow—to snap at the slow-moving cashier, to tap the bumper of the slowpoke ahead of us, or to do something far worse.

5   Technology is also to blame for the bad behavior so widespread in our culture. Amazing gadgets were supposed to make our lives easier—but have they? Sure, technology has its positive aspects. It is a blessing, for instance, to have a cell phone on hand when your car breaks down far from home or to be able to "instant message" a friend on the other side of the globe. But the downsides are many. Cell phones, pagers, fax machines, hand-held computers and the like have robbed many of us of what was once valuable downtime. Now we're always available to take that urgent call or act on that last-minute demand. Then there is the endless pressure of feeling we need to keep up with our gadgets' latest technological developments. For example, it's not sufficient to use your cell phone for phone calls. Now you must learn to use the phone for text-messaging and downloading games. It's not enough to take still photos with your digital

camera. You should know how to shoot ultra high-speed fast-action clips. It's not enough to have an enviable CD collection. You should be downloading new songs in MP3 format. The computers in your house should be connected by a wireless router, and online via high-speed DSL service. In other words, if it's been more than ten minutes since you've updated your technology, you're probably behind.

6   In fact, you're not only behind: you're a stupid loser. At least, that's how most of us end up feeling as we're confronted with more and more unexpected technologies: the do-it-yourself checkout at the supermarket, the telephone "help center" that offers a recorded series of messages, but no human help. And feeling like losers makes us frustrated and, you guessed it, angry. "It's not any one thing but lots of little things that make people feel like they don't have control of their lives," says Jane Middleton-Moz, an author and therapist. "A sense of helplessness is what triggers rage. It's why people end up kicking ATM machines."

7   Tension, the third major culprit behind our epidemic of anger, is intimately connected with our lack of time and the pressures of technology. Merely our chronic exhaustion and our frustration in the face of a bewildering array of technologies would be enough to cause our stress levels to skyrocket, but we are dealing with much more. Our tension is often fueled by a reserve of anger that might be the result of a critical boss, marital discord, or (something that many of today's men and women experience, if few will admit it) a general sense of being stupid and inadequate in the face of the demands of modern life. And along with the challenges of everyday life, we now live with a widespread fear of such horrors as terrorist acts, global warming, and antibiotic-resistant diseases. Our sense of dread may be out of proportion to actual threats because of technology's ability to so constantly bombard us with worrisome information. Twenty-four hours a day news stations bring a stream of horror into our living rooms. As we work on our computers, headlines and graphic images are never more than a mouse-click away.

8   Add it all together—our feeling of never having enough time; the chronic aggravation caused by technology; and our endless, diffuse sense

of stress—and we become time bombs waiting to explode.

Exercise 4 Read the essay above and answer the following questions.

1. Complete the following table.

Introduction (Para(s). _____)	Thesis statement: _____
Cause 1 (Para(s). _____)	Topic sentence: _____ Evidence: 1) _____ 2) _____ 3) _____ 4) _____
Cause 2 (Para(s). _____)	Topic sentence: _____ Evidence: 1) _____ 2) _____ 3) _____
Cause 3 (Para(s). _____)	Topic sentence: _____ Evidence: 1) _____ 2) _____ 3) _____ 4) _____
Conclusion (Para(s). _____)	Which method of conclusion does the text use? A. Summary. B. Thought-provoking question. C. Prediction. D. Recommendation.

2. Does the article achieve unity? State the reasons to support your idea.
   _____
   _____

3. How many examples are given to support the sentence "To begin with, Americans work longer hours and are rewarded with less vacation time than

people in any other industrial society."? Do you think the examples are vivid and clear enough? Why or why not?

_____

_____

4. Find out the transitional signals in three topic sentences.

_____

_____

Writing Practice

Given the prominence of scientific English today, it may seem surprising that no one really knew how to write science in English until the second half of the 17th century. Before that, Latin was regarded as the lingua franca for European intellectuals. There were several reasons why original science continued to be written in Latin instead of English.

The first was simply a matter of audience. Latin was suitable for an international audience of scholars, whereas English reached a socially wider, but more local, audience. Hence, popular science was written in English, but original science was written in Latin.

A second reason for writing in Latin may, perversely, have been a concern for secrecy. Open publication had dangers in putting into the public domain preliminary ideas which had not yet been fully exploited by their "author". As a consequence, scientists felt safer with Latin precisely because its audience, though international, was socially restricted to the "scholars and gentlemen" who understood Latin.

A third reason why the writing of original science in English was delayed may have been to do with the linguistic inadequacy of English in the early modern period. First, it lacked the necessary technical vocabulary. Second, it lacked the grammatical resources required to represent the world in an objective and impersonal way, and to discuss the relations, such as cause and effect, that might hold between complex and hypothetical entities. As a result, English was not well equipped to deal with scientific argument.

Task 1 Read the text above and complete the outline.

Introduction	Thesis statement: _____ _____
Main body	Topic sentence: _____ _____
	Topic sentence: _____ _____
	Topic sentence: _____ _____
Conclusion	Conclusion: _____ _____

Task 2 Answer the following questions.

1. Does the thesis statement indicate the purpose of the text?

2. Which pattern of organization is used in the text to arrange the supporting paragraphs?

3. Does the essay contain transitional signals that indicate a cause or an effect? If so, find them out.

Task 3 Write a cause and effect essay based on the instructions in this section. You can choose one topic from those mentioned in the Introduction or from Exercise 1.

UNIT 6
Environmental Protection

Introduction

Economic development promotes social progress, but it also brings many problems. Among them, environmental problems have attracted worldwide attention. Is the earth getting worse or better? Will fossil fuels run out? The two texts in this unit will help you probe deeper into these questions and contemplate the environmental problems and the use of energy resources.

Learning Objectives

Reading

- Understanding different ideas about the environment
- Learning how to refute an opinion and provide sufficient support for an argument.
- Identifying the essay structure of an environmental study and summarizing the main ideas using topic-related words and phrases
- Developing ideas about environmental problems and solutions to them

Writing

- Learning how to compare and contrast two items
- Using third-person pronouns to express objectively
- Understanding the three formats of a comparison and contrast essay
- Writing a comparison and contrast essay

Unit 6　Environmental Protection

Topic Exploration

Step 1 Use a library catalogue, videos or Internet sources to search for relevant information about environmental problems and environmental protection. Share your findings with your group members.

Step 2 Work in groups to prepare a speech on one of the following topics:
- The environment is getting worse.
- The environment is getting better.

Step 3 One student from each group delivers the speech to the whole class.

Reading

The Truth About the Environment[1]

1　Ecology and economics should push in the same direction. Yet environmentalists and economists are often **at loggerheads**. For economists, the world seems to be getting better. For many environmentalists, it seems to be getting worse. They have developed four

---

1　This text is adapted from "The Truth About the Environment" by Lomborg, B. (2001). *The Economist*, August 4th.

big environmental fears: that natural resources are running out; that the population is ever growing, leaving less and less to eat; that species are becoming extinct in vast numbers, and that the earth's air and water are becoming ever more polluted.

2   But the evidence does not **back** them **up**. First, energy and other natural resources have become more abundant, not less so since the Club of Rome[2] published *The Limits to Growth*[3] in 1972. Second, more food is now produced per head of the world's population than at any time in history and fewer people are starving. Third, although species are indeed becoming extinct, only about 0.7% of them are expected to disappear in the next 50 years, not 25%–50%, as has so often been predicted. And finally, most forms of environmental pollution either appear to have been **overstated**, or are **transient**—associated with the early phases of industrialization and therefore best cured not by restricting economic growth, but by accelerating it. One form of pollution—the release of greenhouse gases that causes global warming—does appear to be a long-term phenomenon, but its total impact is unlikely to pose a **devastating** problem for the future of humanity. A bigger problem may well turn out to be an inappropriate response to it.

3   Take these four points one by one. First, the exhaustion of natural resources. The early environmental movement worried that the mineral resources on which modern industry depends would run out. Clearly, there must be some limit to the amount of fossil fuels and metal **ores** that can be **extracted** from the earth. But that limit is far greater than many environmentalists would have people believe.

4   Next, the population explosion is also turning out to be a **bugaboo**.

---

2 The Club of Rome: an organization of individuals who share a common concern for the future of humanity and strive to make a difference. Its mission is to promote understanding of the global challenges facing humanity and to propose solutions through scientific analysis, communication and advocacy.

3 The Limits to Growth: a 1972 report on the computer simulation of exponential economic and population growth with a finite supply of resources. Funded by the Volkswagen Foundation and commissioned by the Club of Rome, the findings of the study were first presented at international gatherings in Moscow and Rio de Janeiro in the summer of 1971.

Unit 6 Environmental Protection

In 1968, Dr. Ehrlich predicted in his book, *The Population Bomb*[4], that "the battle to feed humanity is over. In the course of the 1970s the world will experience starvation of tragic proportions—hundreds of millions of people will starve to death." However, that did not happen. Instead, according to the United Nations, agricultural production in the developing world has increased by 52% per person since 1961.

5   Third, that threat of biodiversity loss is real, but exaggerated. Most early estimates used simple island models that linked a loss in habitat with a loss of biodiversity. A **rule-of-thumb** indicated that loss of 90% of forest meant a 50% loss of species. Many people expected the number of species to fall by half globally within a generation or two. However, the data simply does not **bear out** these predictions. In the eastern United States, forests were reduced over two centuries to fragments totaling just 1%–2% of their original area, yet this resulted in the extinction of only one forest bird. Yet, when the World Conservation Union[5] and the Brazilian Society of Zoology[6] analyzed all 291 known Atlantic forest animals, none could be declared extinct. Species, therefore, seem more **resilient** than expected.

6   Fourth, pollution is also exaggerated. Many analyses show that air pollution diminishes when a society becomes rich enough to be able to afford to be concerned about the environment. For London, the city for which the best data are available, air pollution peaked around 1890. Today, the air is cleaner than it has been since 1585. There is good reason to believe that this general picture **holds true** for all developed countries. And, although air pollution is increasing in many developing countries, they are merely **replicating** the development of the

---

4 *The Population Bomb*: a best-selling book written by Stanford University Professor Paul R. Ehrlich and his wife, Anne Ehrlich (who was uncredited), in 1968. It warned of mass starvation of humans in the 1970s and 1980s due to overpopulation, as well as other major societal upheavals, and advocated immediate action to limit population growth. Fears of a "population explosion" were widespread in the 1950s and 1960s, but the book and its authors brought the idea to an even wider audience.

5 World Conservation Union: refers to the International Union for Conservation of Nature (IUCN), which was established in 1948. It is an international organization working in the field of nature conservation and sustainable use of natural resources. It involves data gathering and analysis, research, field projects, advocacy, and education.

6 Brazilian Society of Zoology: founded in 1978, is a scientific society devoted to zoology. It publishes the journal *Zoologia*.

industrialized countries.

7   Yet opinion polls suggest that many people **nurture** the belief that environmental standards are declining. Four factors seem to cause this **disjunction** between perception and reality.

8   One is the **lopsidedness** built into scientific research. Scientific funding goes mainly to areas with many problems. That may be wise policy, but it will also create an impression that many more potential problems exist than is the case.

9   Secondly, environmental groups need to be noticed by the mass media. They also need to keep the money rolling in. Understandably, perhaps, they sometimes exaggerate. In 1997, for example, the Worldwide Fund for Nature[7] issued a press release entitled "Two-thirds of the World's Forests Lost Forever". The truth turns out to be nearer 20%.

10   Though these groups are run overwhelmingly by selfless folk, they nevertheless share many of the characteristics of other lobby groups. That would matter less if people applied the same degree of skepticism to environmental lobbying as they do to lobby groups in other fields. A trade organization arguing for, say, weaker pollution controls is instantly seen as self-interested. Yet a green organization opposing such a weakening is seen as **altruistic**.

11   A third source of confusion is the attitude of the media. People are clearly more curious about bad news than good. Newspapers and broadcasters are there to provide what the public wants. That, however, can lead to significant distortions of perception. An example was America's encounter with El Niño in 1997 and 1998. This climatic phenomenon was **accused** of wrecking tourism, causing allergies, melting the ski-slopes and causing 22 deaths by dumping snow in Ohio. However,

---

7   World Wide Fund for Nature: abbreviated as WWF, an international non-governmental organization founded in 1961, working in the field of the wilderness preservation, and the reduction of human impact on the environment. It is the world's largest conservation organization with over five million supporters worldwide, working in more than 100 countries, supporting around 1,300 conservation and environmental projects. Currently, its major work is organized around six areas: food, climate, freshwater, wildlife, forests, and oceans.

according to an article in the *Bulletin of the American Meteorological Society*[8], the damage was estimated at $4 billion. However, the benefits amounted to some $19 billion. These came from higher winter temperatures (which saved an estimated 850 lives, reduced heating costs and diminished spring floods caused by meltwaters). These benefits were not reported as widely as the losses.

12   The fourth factor is poor individual perception. People worry that the endless rise in the amount of stuff everyone throws away will cause the world to run out of places to dispose of waste. Yet, even if America's trash output continues to rise as it has done in the past, and even if the American population doubles by 2100, all the rubbish America produces through the entire 21st century will still take up only one-12,000th of the area of the entire United States.

13   Ignorance matters only when it leads to faulty judgments. But fear of largely imaginary environmental problems can divert political energy from dealing with real ones. It is crucial to look at the facts if people want to make the best possible decisions for the future. It may be costly to be overly optimistic—but more costly still to be too pessimistic.

Words and Phrases

accuse	/əˈkjuːz/	*v.*	to charge with a fault or offense 指控；控告；谴责
		e.g.	Her assistant was accused of theft and fraud by the police.
altruistic	/ˌæltruˈɪstɪk/	*adj.*	having or showing an unselfish concern for the welfare of others 利他的，无私心的
		e.g.	Some may choose to work with vulnerable elderly people for altruistic reasons.
at loggerheads			in or into a state of quarrelsome disagreement 不合，相争

---

8 *Bulletin of the American Meteorological Society*: abbreviated as BAMS, a scientific journal published by the American Meteorological Society (AMS). *BAMS* is the flagship magazine of AMS and publishes peer reviewed articles of interest and significance for the weather, water, and climate community as well as news, editorials, and reviews for AMS members. *BAMS* articles are fully open access. AMS members can also access the digital version which replicates the print issue cover-to-cover and often includes enhanced articles with audio and video.

		e.g.	Councilors were at loggerheads over the grant allocation.
back... up			to support someone or confirm something 支持；证实
		e.g.	U.S. troops were backed up by forces from European countries.
bear out			to prove that something is true 证实，证明
		e.g.	Unhappily the facts do not wholly bear out the theory.
bugaboo	/ˈbʌgəbuː/	*n.*	something that makes people anxious or afraid 妖怪，鬼怪；令人烦恼或恐惧的东西
		e.g.	Red tape is the bugaboo of small businesses.
devastating	/ˈdevəsteɪtɪŋ/	*adj.*	badly damaging or destroying something 毁灭性的；极具破坏性的
		e.g.	The drought has had devastating consequences.
disjunction	/dɪsˈdʒʌŋkʃən/	*n.*	a difference between two things that you would expect to be in agreement 不对应，不一致；脱节
		e.g.	There is a wide disjunction between the cultural norms of his home and community and those of the school.
extract	/ɪkˈstrækt/	*v.*	to remove an object from somewhere, especially with difficulty 取出；提取；获取
		e.g.	After much persuasion they managed to extract the information from him.
hold true			to be valid 适用，有效；保持正确
		e.g.	One thing holds true for all of us: there are no rights without duties.
lopsidedness	/ˌlɒpˈsaɪdɪdnəs/	*n.*	the state of being unequal or uneven, especially in an unfair way 不匀称；不平衡；倾向一方
		e.g.	For decades some economists have criticized the lopsidedness at the core of the U.S. tax system.
nurture	/ˈnɜːtʃə/	*v.*	to help a plan, idea, feeling, etc. to develop 鼓励；培养
		e.g.	The goal of the economic policies is to create jobs and nurture new industries.
ore	/ɔːr/	*n.*	rock or earth from which metal can be obtained 矿石，矿砂
		e.g.	How many tons of ore can this machine crush

Unit 6 Environmental Protection

			in an hour?
overstate	/ˌəʊvəˈsteɪt/	v.	to talk about something in a way that makes it seem more important, serious, etc. than it really is 夸张；夸大；言过其实
		e.g.	The impact of the new legislation has been overstated.
replicate	/ˈreplɪkeɪt/	v.	if you replicate someone's work, a scientific study etc., you do it again, or try to get the same result again 复制；（精确地）仿制
		e.g.	Cells can reproduce but only molecules can replicate.
resilient	/rɪˈzɪliənt/	adj.	able to become strong, happy, or successful again after a difficult situation or event 可迅速恢复的；有适应力的
		e.g.	The company proved remarkably resilient during the recession.
rule-of-thumb		n.	a rough figure or method of calculation, based on practical experience 经验法则，凭经验或实践得来的法则
		e.g.	The designer can use these rule-of-thumb guides to help resolve the confusion.
transient	/ˈtrænziənt/	adj.	continuing only for a short time 短暂的；暂时的
		e.g.	The city has a large transient population.

Reading Comprehension

Task 1 *Text A can be divided into the following four sections. Read the text carefully and work in pairs to find the main idea of each section. Then complete the following table.*

Introduction (Paras. 1–2)	• Many environmentalists fear that natural resources are ____, _____ population keeps _____, many species are _____, and environment on the earth is _____. But that's not necessarily the case because of the following reasons: 1) _____ have become more abundant. 2) _____ and fewer people are starving. 3) _____ is not as serious as being predicted. 4) _____ seems to have been exaggerated.

117

The evidence that the world is not getting worse (Paras. 3–6)	• Natural resources are _____, but _____. • _____ will not cause millions of people _____. Instead, _____ has been on the rise. • Threat of biodiversity loss is overstated, although _____. The data cannot prove that _____. • Air pollution is increasing in many developing countries and they are repeating _____. Analyses show that environmental problem will be a concern when _____, and _____.
Four factors causing the separation between perception and reality (Paras. 7–12)	• The imbalance in _____. Scientific funding will also lead to _____ than is the truth. • _____ need to be noticed by the mass media. • _____ also causes confusion. Media can provide what the public needs, but they may as well cause _____. In some cases _____ were reported widely. • _____ may not be good enough. People fear that there are not enough places _____. Yet, _____.
Conclusion (Para. 13)	• _____ can influence dealing with real problems. It is very important to look at the facts if people want to make the best possible choices for the future. The pay will be great if _____, but it will be more _____.

Task 2 Based on the information in Task 1, write a summary of the text in 80–100 words. Try to make your paragraph logical and coherent.

Task 3 Work in groups to discuss the following questions.

1. What's the author's attitude towards environmental problems? Is it optimistic or pessimistic?

2. Why does the author think the attitude of the media is one factor that confuses people's perceptions of environmental problems?

3. "It may be costly to be overly optimistic—but more costly still to be too pessimistic." How do you understand the statement at the end of the last paragraph?

4. Are you optimistic or pessimistic about the environmental problems? State your reasons.

Unit 6 Environmental Protection

5. What do you think you can do to make the earth less polluted?

Vocabulary

Task 1 For each sentence there are four choices marked A, B, C, and D. Choose the one that best keeps the meaning with the underlined part.

1. I thought places like this were extinct in our district, Linda said. She lit a cigarette and began to smoke.

   A. died out   B. exited   C. exhausted   D. extended

2. I realized that this idea had always been at the back of my mind: that everything in his life was transient.

   A. transparent   B. transitive   C. temporary   D. transferable

3. We've seen our house diminish greatly in value over the last six months.

   A. destroy   B. reduce   C. refund   D. devalue

4. We have several professional comedians in our club, and I've been amazed at just how much humor they're able to extract from our meetings.

   A. process   B. produce   C. obtain   D. obey

5. He said the European Union, which France currently heads, could not allow such a terribly devastating and unacceptable war.

   A. defensive   B. dangerous   C. decaying   D. destructive

6. The authors no doubt overstated their case with a view to catching the public's attention.

   A. overcame   B. exaggerated   C. claimed   D. described

7. Radio signals received from the galaxy's center back up the black hole theory.

   A. light up   B. retreat   C. support   D. rebut

8. The medium that carries your marketing message must be easy to transfer and replicate: e-mail, website, graphic, software download.

   A. remove   B. resume   C. revive   D. reproduce

9. Nurture your mind with great thoughts, for you will never go any higher than you think.

   A. Develop   B. Capture   C. Educate   D. Deduce

10. The nature of a state is a social man rather than an economic man, with a dualism of being both self-interested and altruistic.

   A. trustful   B. unselfish   C. selfish   D. humanly

Task 2 Complete the following sentences with the words and phrases given below. Change the form if necessary.

overly	resilient	lopsided	disjunction
rule-of-thumb	bear out	at loggerheads	divert
hold true	amount to		

1. The first election under the new constitution has left its two big ideas _____.

2. Breaking through the confines and realizing the modern childbearing culture, it needs to change the old custom of unilateral _____ in matrimony and family.

3. A good _____ is that a broker must generate sales of ten times his salary.

4. They want to _____ the attention of the people from the real issues.

5. If your business expenses _____ less than 52% of your gross business income, you are "not very likely" to get audited.

6. She is very _____ to change.

7. Their arguments were valid a hundred years ago and they still _____ today.

8. He was acting out his feelings of inferiority by being _____ aggressive.

9. But the _____ between the strengthening U.S. and the rest of the world is deepening.

10. Recent studies _____ claims that perfumes can cause psychological changes.

Unit 6　**Environmental Protection**

Translation

Task 1　Translate the following paragraph into Chinese.

　　Ignorance matters only when it leads to faulty judgments. But fear of largely imaginary environmental problems can divert political energy from dealing with real ones. It is crucial to look at the facts if people want to make the best possible decisions for the future. It may be costly to be overly optimistic—but more costly still to be too pessimistic.

Task 2　Translate the following paragraph into English with the help of the words in brackets.

　　在波多黎各，原始森林的面积在过去的 400 年间减少了 99%。然而，60 种鸟类中只有 7 个灭绝了——根据经验法则，应该是一半的鸟类都会灭绝。对风险的错误认识可能付出更高的代价。理性的环境管理和环境投资是不错的想法，但是这种投资的成本和收益应该与人类活动在其他重要领域内的类似投资相比较。（reduce, extinct, rule-of-thumb, perception, lead to）

Text B　**Using Waste, Swedish City Cuts Its Fossil Use**

Read **Text B** online and do the exercises.

Comparison and Contrast Essay

Introduction

The purpose of a comparison and contrast essay is to analyze the similarities and/or differences between two subjects. The process of comparing and contrasting two ideas, objects, theories, or phenomena is an indispensable part of academic study. It enables us to analyze two different subjects on a deeper level and then thoroughly understand the subjects. This type of essay is very challenging because it requires not only a full understanding of two different subjects, but also a clear explanation of the reasons for the comparison.

Exercise 1 List some comparison and contrast essay topics related to your major with your partner. The first three are examples.

- Hatred and love, how these topics are treated in the *Hamlet*?
- Living on campus and living off campus, which is better?
- The differences and similarities between the two movies—*The Godfather* and *Once upon a Time in America*.
- _____
- _____
- _____
- _____

Features of a Comparison and Contrast Essay

Below are the features of a comparison and contrast essay.

Thesis statement	• Present the purpose (comparison or contrast or a combination of both) of the essay. • Explain why it's meaningful to compare these two subjects.
Be objective	• First, use the third-person pronouns instead of the first-person and the second-person pronouns. • Second, use solid evidence to support your opinion, and avoid making biased comments.
Transitional signals	• Signals that show comparison, such as *like, similar to, similarly, by analogy, likewise, in the same way, in the same manner, the same as, equally important, at the same time…* • Signals that show contrast, such as *unlike, conversely, on the contrary, whereas, instead, but, compared to, correspondingly, as well as, both, too, in addition, on the one hand… on the other hand…*

Exercise 2 Read the essay below and answer the questions about the features of a comparison and contrast essay.

Frogs and Toads: Alike but Different

Most of the people find it difficult to differentiate a frog from a toad. They normally mix them up. Although they seem so similar in appearance, they certainly have numerous dissimilarities too.

Frogs are found in many different shapes, sizes, colours, and textures. Frogs have smooth, wet skin. They live most of the time in or near water. They have different eye colours including brown, silver, green, gold and red along with different shapes and sizes of pupils. Some of the frogs have sticky padding on their feet while others have webbed feet. It is obvious that not even all the frogs have same qualities.

Toads too have numerous shapes, sizes, and texture, but they don't have much variety in colour. Toads are chubby and have warty skin. They do spend most of their time in water, but they live in moist places like woods, fields and gardens. Their pupils do have different shapes, sizes, and colours, but generally they are egg-shaped, small and black. Usually they have webbed feet.

Toads and frogs have the same way to catch and eat food. Both of them use their tongue to gulp down the prey. But a frog has a crest of very small cone teeth around the upper jaw edge to seize the food, but a toad doesn't have any teeth at all. They eat almost the same foods as frogs like bugs, insects, fish, etc.

To sum up, frogs and toads do seem similar but they have several different qualities regarding shape, size, colour, and texture. Therefore, it is crystal clear that people mistake while figuring out the difference between a frog and a toad. It is needed that one should learn how a frog differs from a toad.

1. Does this essay have a thesis statement? Is it a good one?
_____
_____

2. Do you think the tone of this essay is objective? Why?
_____
_____

3. Find the transitional signals that indicate comparison and contrast in this essay.
_____
_____

Format of a Comparison and Contrast Essay

There are generally three types of formats of a comparison and contrast essay.

Subject-to-subject	Point-by-point	Compare then contrast
Introduction	Introduction	Introduction
Main body	**Main body**	**Main body**
Subject A	Point 1	Comparison of Subject A
Point 1	Subject A	& Subject B
Point 2	Subject B	Comparison 1
Point 3	Point 2	Comparison 2
Subject B	Subject A	Comparison 3
Point 1	Subject B	Contrast of Subject A &
Point 2	Point 3	Subject B
Point 3	Subject A	Contrast 1
Conclusion	Subject B	Contrast 2
	Conclusion	Contrast 3
		Conclusion

The introduction part should begin with the topics to be compared and contrasted and end with a thesis statement. The body paragraphs are the arguments that support your thesis statement. Each body paragraph should begin with a topic sentence to clearly state the argument, and the topic sentence is followed by specific and solid evidence. In the conclusion part, you may summarize the main idea of the text, reemphasize the significance of comparing and contrasting the two subjects, and make a prediction or some final comments.

- **Subject-to-subject format**

In this format, the first part of the main body fully discusses all the points of subject A that you want to compare or contrast, and the second part deals entirely with the points of subject B, which should follow the same order as those of subject A. For example, if you want to contrast the differences between two universities and help people make a better choice, you may list the features of University A, such as the campus, school location, majors and the faculty. Then, you list the corresponding features of University B. Make sure the features of each side are listed in the same order, so that readers can understand the overall situation quickly and clearly. Look at the outline below.

Subject-to-subject format
Thesis statement: University A and University B are both great choices, but they differ in terms of the campus, school location, and majors and the faculty.

Main body
    Subject A
        Point 1 (Campus)
        Point 2 (School location)
        Point 3 (Majors and the faculty)
    Subject B
        Point 1 (Campus)
        Point 2 (School location)
        Point 3 (Majors and the faculty)
Conclusion

- **Point-by-point format**

In this format, the main body consists of several paragraphs which compare or contrast subject A and subject B point by point. For example, in contrasting two universities, you can first discuss the campus of these two universities, then the location, and finally majors and the faculty. Look at the outline below.

Point-by-point format

Thesis statement: University A and University B are both great choices, but they differ in terms of the campus, school location, and majors and the faculty.
Main body
  Point 1 (Campus)
    Subject A (University A)
    Subject B (University B)
  Point 2 (School location)
    Subject A (University A)
    Subject B (University B)
  Point 3 (Majors and the faculty)
    Subject A (University A)
    Subject B (University B)
Conclusion

- **Compare then contrast format**

The body part of this format first discusses the similarities between two subjects, and then explains the differences between them. For example, you can first discuss the similarities between University A and University B, and then turn to their differences. The points discussed in the comparison part can be the same as those in the contrast part. For example, you can compare and contrast two universities in terms of the campus, school location, and majors and the faculty. Meanwhile, the points discussed in the comparison part can also be different from those in the contrast part. For example, you can compare two universities from aspects of school history, school ranking, and academic atmosphere, and then contrast them from aspects of the campus, school location, majors and the faculty.

Compare then contrast format
Thesis statement: University A and University B are both great universities with several similarities, but they also differ in terms of the campus, school location, and majors and the faculty. **Main body** 　Comparison of Subject A and Subject B (University A and University B) 　　Comparison 1(Campus) or (Another feature) 　　Comparison 2 (School location) or (Another feature) 　　Comparison 3 (Majors and the faculty) or (Another feature) 　Contrast of Subject A and Subject B (University A and University B) 　　Contrast 1 (Campus) 　　Contrast 2 (School location) 　　Contrast 3 (Majors and the faculty) **Conclusion**

Exercise 3　Choose one of the topics you have discussed in the Introduction part and Exercise 1. Develop the topic into three formats of compare and contrast essay, and write down the outline of each of the format.

Subject-to-subject	Point-by-point	Compare then contrast

Sample Essay Analysis

Understanding the Differences Between Men and Women

1　For centuries, the differences between men and women were socially defined and distorted through a lens of sexism in which men assumed superiority over women and maintained it through domination. As the goal of equality between men and women now grows closer, we are also losing our awareness of important differences. In some circles of society, politically correct thinking is obliterating important discussion as well as our awareness of the similarities and differences between men and women. The vision of equality between the sexes has narrowed the possibilities for discovery of what truly exists within a man and within a woman. The world is less interesting when everything is same.

2   It is my position that men and women are equal but different. When I say equal, I mean that men and women have a right to equal opportunity and protection under the law. The fact that people in this country are assured these rights does not negate my observation that men and women are at least as different psychologically as they are physically.

3   None of us would argue the fact that men and women are physically different. The physical differences are rather obvious and most of these can be seen and easily measured. Weight, shape, size and anatomy are not political opinions but rather tangible and easily measured. The physical differences between men and women provide functional advantages and have survival value. Men usually have greater upper body strength, build muscle easily, have thicker skin, bruise less easily and have a lower threshold of awareness of injuries to their extremities. Men are essentially built for physical confrontation and the use of force. Their joints are well suited for throwing objects. A man's skull is almost always thicker and stronger than a woman's. The stereotype that men are more "thick-headed" than women is not far-fetched. A man's "thick-headedness", and other anatomical differences have been associated with a uniquely male attraction to high speed activities and reckless behavior that usually involve collisions with other males or automobiles. Men invented the game "chicken", not women. Men, and a number of other male species of animals seem to charge and crash into each other a great deal in their spare time.

4   Women, on the other hand, have four times as many brain cells (neurons) connecting the right and left side of their brain. This latter finding provides physical evidence that supports the observation that men rely easily and more heavily on their left brain to solve one problem one step at a time. Women have more efficient access to both sides of their brain and therefore greater use of their right brain. Women can focus on more than one problem at one time and frequently prefer to

solve problems through multiple activities at a time. Nearly every parent has observed how young girls find the conversations of young boys "boring". Young boys express confusion and would rather play sports than participate actively in a conversation between 5 girls who are discussing as many as three subjects at once!

5   The psychological differences between man and women are less obvious. They can be difficult to describe. Yet these differences can profoundly influence how we form and maintain relationships that can range from work and friendships to marriage and parenting.

6   Recognizing, understanding, discussing as well as acting skillfully in light of the differences between men and women can be difficult. Our failure to recognize and appreciate these differences can become a lifelong source of disappointment, frustration, tension and eventually our downfall in a relationship. Not only can these differences destroy a promising relationship, but most people will grudgingly accept or learn to live with the consequences. Eventually they find some compromise or way to cope. Few people ever work past these difficulties. People tend to accept what they don't understand when they feel powerless to change it.

7   Relationships between men and women are not impossible or necessarily difficult. Problems simply arise when we expect or assume the opposite sex should think, feel or act the way we do. It's not that men and women live in completely different realities. Rather, our lack of knowledge and mutual experience gives rise to our difficulties.

8   Despite great strides in this country toward equality, modern society hasn't made relationships between men and women any easier. Today's society has taught us and has imposed on us the expectation that men and women should live together continuously, in communion, and in harmony. These expectations are not only unrealistic but ultimately, they leave people feeling unloved, inadequate, cynical, apathetic or ashamed. The challenge facing men and women is to become aware of their identities, to accept their differences, and to live their lives fully and as skillfully as possible. To do this we must first understand in what ways we are different. We must avoid trying to change others to suit our needs.

Exercise 4 Read the essay above and answer the following questions.

1. Which format is adopted in this essay?
   _____
   _____

2. Complete the outline of this essay.

Introduction (Para(s). _____)	Thesis statement: _____
Main body (Para(s). _____)	Point 1: _____ (Para(s). _____) Topic sentence: _____ Point 2: _____ (Para(s). _____) Topic sentence: _____
Conclusion (Para(s). _____)	Methods used in the conclusion part: _____

3. Do you think the thesis statement of this essay is a good one? If not, rewrite one.
   _____
   _____

4. Do you think the author has fully discussed the psychological differences between men and women?
   _____
   _____

Writing Practice

Task Develop one of the outlines you write in Exercise 3 into a comparison and contrast essay in no less than 200 words.

UNIT 7

History

Introduction

Histories make men wise; poets, witty. History connects us with our ancestors. The historical rites and relics displayed in museums are all good proofs of history. Museums are special places to tell history vividly in non-written form. Through these ancient but precious objects, we can see the social development and culture behind them. Who dug up these treasures from the ruins and mausoleums? It is the archeologist. What do you know about archeology? In this unit, you'll read two texts which might help you learn more about museums and archeology.

Learning Objectives

Reading

- Understanding the historical development of museums
- Recognizing the significance of archeology
- Cultivating patriotism in learning history
- Summarizing historical events with topic-related words and phrases

Writing

- Understanding different patterns of opinion essays
- Writing an effective thesis statement
- Identifying main arguments and supporting details in an opinion essay
- Using formal and objective language in an opinion essay
- Writing an outline of an opinion essay

Unit 7 History

Topic Exploration

Step 1 Watch the documentary *The Palace Museum* presented by CCTV-1, with 2 episodes for each group. Take notes to summarize the main plot of each episode.

Step 2 Work in groups to exchange notes and make a PowerPoint presentation to sum up the main idea of the two episodes, especially the important historical events. You can report the events in time order.

Step 3 Each group makes a presentation of your result to the whole class.

Reading

The Development of Museums[1]

1   The **conviction** that historical relics provide **infallible** testimony about the past is rooted in the nineteenth and early twentieth centuries, when science was regarded as objective and value free. As one writer observes: "Although it is now evident that artifacts are as easily altered as chronicles, public faith in their **veracity** endures: a tangible relic seems ipso facto real." Such conviction was, until recently, reflected in

---

1   This text is adapted from *Heritage, Tourism and Society* by Herbert, D. T. (1997). London: Continuum.

museum displays. Museums used to look—and some still do—much like storage rooms of objects packed together in showcases: good for scholars who wanted to study the subtle differences in design, but not for the ordinary visitor, to whom it all looked alike. Similarly, the information accompanying the objects often made little sense to the lay visitor. The content and format of explanations dated back to a time when the museum was the exclusive domain of the scientific researcher.

2 Recently, however, attitudes towards history and the way it should be presented have altered. The key word in heritage display is now "experience", the more exciting the better and, if possible, involving all the senses. Good examples of this approach in the UK are the Jorvik Centre[2] in York; the National Museum of Photography[3], Film and Television in Bradford; and the **Imperial** War Museum in London. In the U.S. the trend emerged much earlier: Williamsburg[4] has been a **prototype** for many heritage developments in other parts of the world. No one can predict where the process will end. On so-called heritage sites the **re-enactment** of historical events is increasingly popular, and computers will soon provide virtual reality experiences, which will present visitors with a vivid image of the period of their choice, in which they themselves can act as if part of the historical environment. Such developments have been criticized as an intolerable **vulgarization**, but the success of many historical theme parks and similar locations suggests that the majority of the public does not share this opinion.

3 In a related development, the sharp distinction between museum and heritage sites on the one hand, and theme parks on the other, is gradually evaporating. They already borrow ideas and concepts from one

---

2 Jorvik Centre: an award-winning museum that recreates in vivid detail the sights, smells, sounds, and flavor of daily life in the tumultuous world of 10th-century York. Jorvik recreates the Viking world through a series of tableaux depicting markets, shops, streets scenes, and other aspects of daily life, including meal preparation and the ever-popular latrine scene.

3 National Museum of Photography: It got its name in 1996 and holds a large collection of photographs. The collections are kept in storage with no permanent exhibition, but the museum organizes changing temporary exhibitions of varying themes and artists.

4 Williamsburg: a famous tourist city in U.S. with many historical relics. It was the state capital of Virginia from 1699, when it was renamed in honor of William III, until 1799, when Richmond became the capital.

another. For example, museums have adopted story lines for exhibitions, sites have accepted "theming" as a relevant tool, and theme parks are moving towards more **authenticity** and research-based presentations. In zoos, animals are no longer kept in cages, but in great spaces, either in the open air or in enormous greenhouses, such as the jungle and desert environments in Burgers' Zoo[5] in Holland. This particular trend is regarded as one of the major developments in the presentation of natural history in the twentieth century.

4   Theme parks are undergoing other changes, too, as they try to present more serious social and cultural issues, and move away from fantasy. This development is a response to market forces and, although museums and heritage sites have a special, rather distinct role to fulfill, they are also operating in a very competitive environment, where visitors make choices on how and where to spend their free time. Heritage and museum experts do not have to invent stories and recreate historical environments to attract their visitors: their assets are already in place. However, exhibits must be both based on artifacts and facts as we know them, and attractively presented. Those who are professionally engaged in the art of interpreting history are thus in a difficult position, as they must **steer** a narrow course between the demands of "evidence" and "attractiveness" especially given the increasing need in the heritage industry for income-generating activities.

5   It could be claimed that in order to make everything in heritage more "real", historical accuracy must be increasingly altered. For example, Pithecanthropus erectus[6] is depicted in an Indonesian museum with Malay facial features, because this **corresponds to** public perceptions. Similarly, in the Museum of Natural History in Washington, Neanderthal

---

5 Burgers' Zoo: Unlike traditional zoos, Burgers' Zoo has eco-displays, where large scale natural habitats are recreated in which animals, nature and visitor roam together. In 1988, one and a half hectares of tropical rainforest (the Bush) was opened to the public.

6 Pithecanthropus erectus: extinct hominin (member of the human lineage) known from fossil remains found on the island of Java, Indonesia. A skullcap and femur (thighbone) discovered by the Dutch anatomist and geologist Eugène Dubois in the early 1890s were the first known fossils of the species Homo erectus.

man[7] is shown making a dominant gesture to his wife. Such presentations tell us more about **contemporary** perceptions of the world than about our ancestors. There is one compensation, however, for the professionals who make these interpretations: if they did not provide the interpretation, visitors would do it for themselves, based on their own ideas, misconceptions and prejudices. And no matter how exciting the result is, it would contain a lot more bias than the presentations provided by experts.

6 Human bias is **inevitable**, but another source of bias in the representation of history has to do with the **transitory** nature of the materials themselves. The simple fact is that not everything from history survives the historical process. Castles, palaces and cathedrals have a longer lifespan than the dwellings of ordinary people. The same applies to the furnishings and other contents of the **premises**. In a town like Leyden in Holland, which in the seventeenth century was occupied by approximately the same number of inhabitants as today, people lived within the walled town, an area more than five times smaller than modern Leyden. In most of the houses several families lived together in circumstances beyond our imagination. Yet in museums, fine period rooms give only an image of the lifestyle of the upper class of that era. No wonder that people who **stroll** around exhibitions are filled with **nostalgia**; the evidence in museums indicates that life was so much better in the past. This notion is **induced** by the bias in its representation in museums and heritage centers.

Words and Phrases

authenticity /ˌɔːθenˈtɪsəti/ *n.* the quality of being real or true 真实性，确实性；可靠性
e.g. The film's authenticity of detail has impressed critics.

contemporary /kənˈtempərəri/ *adj.* belonging to the present time 当代的；同时代的
e.g. Perhaps he should have a more updated look, a more contemporary style.

---

7 Neanderthal man: Neanderthals are an extinct species of hominids that were the closest relatives to modern human beings. They lived throughout Europe and parts of Asia from about 400,000 until about 40,000 years ago, and they were adept at hunting large, Ice Age animals.

conviction	/kənˈvɪkʃən/	n.	a very strong belief or opinion 确信；信念
		e.g.	She was motivated by deep religious conviction.
correspond to			to be very similar to or the same as something else 相称；相当于
		e.g.	The written record of the conversation doesn't correspond to what was actually said.
imperial	/ɪmˈpɪəriəl/	adj.	relating to an empire or to the person who rules it 帝国的；至高无上的
		e.g.	The glittering ceremony conjured up images of Russia's imperial past.
induce	/ɪnˈdjuːs/	v.	to persuade someone to do something, especially something that does not seem wise 诱导；引起
		e.g.	Patients with eating disorders may use drugs to induce vomiting.
inevitable	/ɪˈnevətəbəl/	adj.	certain to happen and impossible to avoid 必然的，不可避免的
		e.g.	Since the leaders can't agree, more fighting is inevitable.
infallible	/ɪnˈfæləbəl/	adj.	always right and never making mistakes 一贯正确的；万无一失的
		e.g.	These believers say Apple's judgment on the market is nearly infallible.
nostalgia	/nɒˈstældʒə/	n.	a feeling that a time in the past was good, or the activity of remembering a good time in the past and wishing that things had not changed 怀旧，念旧
		e.g.	Some people feel nostalgia for their schooldays.
premises	/ˈpremɪs/	n.	the buildings and land that a shop, restaurant, company, etc. uses（企业的）房屋建筑及附属场地；营业场所
		e.g.	The company is looking for larger premises.
prototype	/ˈprəʊtətaɪp/	n.	a first or preliminary version of a device or vehicle from which other forms are developed 原型；标准，模范
		e.g.	The firm is testing a prototype of the weapon.
re-enactment	/ˌriːɪˈnæktmənt/	n.	an activity that repeats the actions of a past event, especially as an entertainment（对事件的）再现，重现
		e.g.	He claimed that this was not a re-enactment of existing law.

steer	/stɪə/	v.	guide someone's behavior or the way a situation develops 控制，引导
		e.g.	Teachers try to steer pupils away from drugs.
stroll	/strəʊl/	v.	to walk somewhere in a slow relaxed way 漫步；闲逛
		e.g.	People were strolling along the beach.
transitory	/ˈtrænzətəri/	adj.	continuing or existing for only a short time 短暂的，暂时的
		e.g.	Most teenage romances are transitory.
veracity	/vəˈræsəti/	n.	the fact of being true or correct 真实，准确；诚实
		e.g.	We have total confidence in the veracity of our research.
vulgarization	/ˌvʌlɡəraɪˈzeɪʃən/	n.	the act of rendering something coarse and unrefined 通俗化；粗俗化
		e.g.	The vulgarization of TV drama is the combined effect of the entire circulation.

Reading Comprehension

Task 1 Text A can be divided into the following three sections. Read the text carefully and work in pairs to find the main idea of each section. Then complete the following table.

Museum display in the past (Para. 1)	• Museums used to look—and some still do—much like _____ _____ in showcases: good for _____ _____ who wanted to study the subtle differences in design, but not for the _____, to whom it all looked alike.
Recent changes on heritage display (Paras. 2–5)	• The key word in heritage display is now _____ _____, the more _____ the better and, if possible, involving all the senses. • In a related development, the sharp distinction between museum and heritage sites on the one hand, and theme parks on the other, is gradually _____. 1) Museums have adopted _____ for exhibitions. 2) Sites have accepted _____ as a relevant tool. 3) Theme parks are moving towards more _____ and _____.

138

| Inevitable bias (Para. 6) | • Human bias is inevitable, but another source of bias in the representation of history has to do with the _____ _____. |

Task 2 Based on the information in Task 1, write a summary of the text in 80–100 words. Try to make your paragraph logical and coherent.

Task 3 Work in groups to discuss the following questions.

1. Why does the author say museums are much like storage rooms of objects?
2. What are the changes on theme parks?
3. Why does the writer say the bias is inevitable?
4. Do you like to go to museums? What kind of museums do you like most? Why?
5. What's the most memorable museum you've been to? What impressed you the most about it?

Vocabulary

Task 1 For each sentence there are four choices marked A, B, C, and D. Choose the one that best keeps the meaning with the underlined part.

1. They questioned the veracity of her story.

   A. truth   B. evidence   C. fact   D. authority

2. There should be some tangible evidence that the economy is starting to recover.

   A. sufficient   B. real   C. positive   D. profound

3. Scientists have developed a working prototype for the machine.

   A. principle   B. protocol   C. model   D. procedure

4. In a unique visual point, *Gone with the Wind* provides us something about the civil war and the inevitable tragedy of the dominant class.

   A. invisible   B. incapable   C. unbelievable   D. unavoidable

5. Nothing will <u>induce</u> me to vote for him again.

   A. introduce   B. tell   C. persuade   D. induct

6. There is enough history left to get a sense of the old city as you <u>stroll</u>.

   A. walk   B. explore   C. discover   D. search

7. Racegoers will be given a number which will <u>correspond to</u> a horse running in a race.

   A. according to   B. respond to   C. correlate to   D. match

8. Although he was experienced, he was not <u>infallible</u>.

   A. faultless   B. infinite   C. foolish   D. promising

9. His explanations have invariably emphasized the <u>transitory</u> nature of the problem.

   A. transitive   B. practical   C. temporary   D. complicated

10. There was a sense of <u>nostalgia</u> in the mind of the domestic immigrants, so they always gathered in groups to seek developments.

    A. homesickness   B. missing   C. longing   D. desire

Task 2 Complete the following sentences with the words and phrases given below. Change the form if necessary.

testimony	steer	conviction	heritage
date back	imperial	contemporary	
authentic	apply to	no wonder that	

1. Americans held the _____ that anyone could become rich if they worked hard.

2. History is full of attempts at _____ domination.

3. The community's links with Syria _____ to biblical times.

4. These works of art are considered of great importance to Russia's national _____.

5. Helen tried to _____ the conversation away from herself.

Unit 7 **History**

6. Buttons and switches were clearly numbered to _____ a chart on the wall.

7. Archaeological evidence may help to establish the _____ of the statue.

8. The judge would not admit the _____, ruling that it was extrinsic to the matter at hand.

9. With little or no previous experience, it is _____ you start to fumble.

10. Since its opening in 1978, the gallery has been seen as the main center for _____ art in the city.

Translation

Task 1 *Translate the following paragraph into Chinese.*

Museums used to look—and some still do—much like storage rooms of objects packed together in showcases: good for scholars who wanted to study the subtle differences in design, but not for the ordinary visitor, to whom it all looked alike. Similarly, the information accompanying the objects often made little sense to the lay visitor. The content and format of explanations dated back to a time when the museum was the exclusive domain of the scientific researcher.

Task 2 *Translate the following paragraph into English with the help of the words in brackets.*

社会发展和科技进步使得博物馆正在不断被重新定义。博物馆已不仅是收藏、保护、研究、展示文化遗产的机构，还成为服务人的全面发展、面向未来的文化服务和教育机构。目前，中国博物馆正在经历着"以物为本"向"以人为本"的观念转变，博物馆作为公共文化服务机构的属性不断强化，工作重点不再是博物馆的科技性，而是调整博物馆与公众之间的关系，更好地满足公众教育和文化消费方面的需求。（heritage, alter, adjust）

Text B

The Nature and Aims of Archeology

Read **Text B** online and do the exercises.

Writing Focus

Opinion Essay

Introduction

Opinion essay is a common type of academic writing. Its purpose is to present a standpoint about an issue and attempt to convince the reader by extensive research of the issue and detailed study of the supporting evidence. A successful opinion essay is like an inspiring movie which may change a reader's stance. Just as the audiences are inspired by the reasonable and impressive plots of a movie, the readers are usually persuaded by the valid arguments and solid supporting evidence in an opinion essay.

Patterns of an Opinion Essay

An opinion essay usually consists of three parts: the introduction which introduces the background of the topic and reveals the author's viewpoint—thesis statement, the body which is the most important part and often contains several arguments to support the main idea, and finally the conclusion which may summarize or restate the author's stance and may inspire the readers to learn more about the issue under discussion. To make his ideas more objective and persuasive, the writer sometimes would present opposite opinions and give targeted rebuttals. If the counter-arguments are presented, two common patterns may be used to organize the essay as follows:

Pattern 1	Pattern 2

Introduction
  A. Background of the topic
  B. Thesis statement
Body paragraphs
  A. Argument 1
    a. Supporting evidence 1
    b. Supporting evidence 2
  B. Argument 2
    a. Supporting evidence 1
    b. Supporting evidence 2
  C. Argument 3
    a. Supporting evidence 1
    b. Supporting evidence 2
  D. Counter-arguments and rebuttals
Conclusion
	Introduction
	  A. Background of the topic
	  B. Thesis statement
	Body paragraphs
	  A. Counter-argument 1
	    Rebuttal 1
	  B. Counter-argument 2
	    Rebuttal 2
	  C. Counter-argument 3
	    Rebuttal 3
	Conclusion

The differences between the two patterns lie in the body part. If the writer emphasizes on presenting his own understanding and judgments about the issue, Pattern 1 is often preferred, with supporting evidence given to justify each argument, thereby backing up the thesis statement. In Pattern 1, counter-arguments sometimes are not presented. In Pattern 2, counter-arguments are highlighted and each is given rebuttals to illustrate the writer's position. This pattern may be used when the popular beliefs stand against the writer's point of view.

Features of an Opinion Essay

1. The introduction with a good thesis statement

A good introduction, which may include more than one paragraph, usually can attract readers' attention and inform them of the main idea with a proper thesis statement summarizing the writer's position. The thesis statement should be neither too specific nor too general. An excessively specific thesis statement may not provoke further arguments to illuminate the idea; it may just serve as a fact rather than a viewpoint. If the thesis statement is too general, the supporting paragraphs may incorporate information which is not closely related to the main idea. Two parts are included in a proper thesis statement—topic and controlling idea.

Here are some examples:

Thesis statement	Topic	Controlling idea
There are many reasons why pollution in ABC Town is the worst in the world.	Pollution in ABC Town is the worst in the world.	Many reasons
Teen pregnancy may be prevented by improved education.	Teen pregnancy may be prevented.	Improved education

2. Authoritative and persuasive supporting evidence

How can readers be persuaded by an opinion essay? General arguments and ideas are not enough. They are like the roof of a house which needs props to hold its weight. In a successful opinion essay, ideas are well illustrated and backed up by supporting evidence, which helps the readers to examine the arguments and make judgments about their validity. Supporting evidence is an effective tool for the writer to convey ideas that may convince the readers.

3. Formal and objective language

Formal and objective language is also necessary for a successful opinion essay, especially in academic writing. Informal and colloquial words ought to be avoided. Complex and compound sentences, which are more informative, are preferred. The second person and the first person pronouns like "you", "your", "we" and "I" should be avoided. Contractions such as "don't", "won't", "isn't" should not be used. Coordinating conjunctions such as "and", "but" and "so" should not be placed at the beginning of a sentence. Nominalization and passive voice are used to avoid personal expressions and emotions.

Exercise 1 Answer the following questions about the features of an opinion essay.

1. What are the functions of the introduction part?

_____

_____

2. How do we write a good introduction in an opinion essay? What should be written in this part?

   _____
   _____

3. What can be used as supporting evidence in an opinion essay?

   _____
   _____

4. Tick the features authoritative and persuasive supporting evidence bears.

   _____ clearly stated sources

   _____ focusing on related aspects of the thesis statement

   _____ specific

   _____ adequate

   _____ accurate

   _____ richly textured and fresh rather than overused

Sample Essay Analysis

Separating the Sexes, Just for the Tough Years

The middle school years are known to be the "tough years". These are the years when the uneven pace of girls' and boys' physical, emotional, and cognitive development is most noticeable. Girls are ahead of boys and girls during these difficult years might improve their academic performance. Separating classes are now prohibited in public schools that receive government funds, but a change is under consideration. Although some parents and educators oppose same-sex classes, there is some evidence that separating boys and girls in middle school yields positive results.

Opponents of single-sex education claim that test scores of students in all-girl or all-boy classes are no higher than those of students in mixed classes ("Study", 1998). However, the research is inconclusive. Despite the fact that some research shows no improvement in test scores, other research shows exactly opposite results (Blum, 2002). More importantly, many psychologists believe that test scores are the wrong measuring sticks. They believe that self-confidence and self-esteem issues are more important than test scores. In same-sex classes, girls report increased confidence ("Study", 1998). These are results that cannot be calculated by a test but that will help adolescents become successful adults long after the difficult years of middle school are past. New York University professor Carol Gilligan is certain that girls are more likely to be "creative thinkers and risk-takers as adults if educated apart from boys"(Cross, 2004). Boys, too, gain confidence when they do not have to compete with girls. With no girls in the classroom, they are more at ease with themselves and more receptive to learning (Cross, 2004).

Opponents also maintain that separating classes send the message that males and females cannot work together. They say that when students go into the work force, they will have to work side-by-side with the opposite sex and attending all-girl or all-boy schools denies them the opportunities to learn how to do so ("North", 2000). However, such an argument completely ignores the fact that children constantly interact with members of the opposite sex outside schools. From playing and squabbling with siblings to negotiating allowances, chores, and privileges with their opposite-sex parent, children learn and practice on daily basis the skills they will need in their future workplaces.

The final argument advanced by opponents of same-sex education is that it is discriminatory and therefore, unconstitutional. However, research supports exactly the opposite conclusion: that discrimination is widespread in mixed classes. Several studies have shown that boys dominate discussions and receive more attention than girls and that teachers call on boys more often than they call on girls, even when girls raise their hands ("North", 2000). Clearly, this is discriminatory.

It should be evident that the arguments against same-sex classes are not valid. On the contrary, many people involved in middle-school education say that same-sex classes provide a better learning environment. Boys and girls pay less attention to each other and more attention to their schoolwork (Marquez, 2004). As one teacher noted, "Girls are more relaxed and ask more questions; boys are less disruptive and more focused" ("North", 2000). Furthermore, schoolchildren are not disadvantaged by lack of contact with the opposite sex because they have many opportunities outside the school setting to interact with one another. Finally, discrimination which often occurs in mixed classes won't take place in the same-sex classes.

Source: Oshima, A. & Hogue, A. (2006). *Writing Academic English* (4th ed.). New York: Pearson Education.

References

Blum, J. (2002). Scores Soar at D.C. School with Same-Sex Classes. *The Washington Post*, June 27.

Gross, J. (2004). Splitting Up Boys and Girls, Just for the Tough Years. *The New York Times*, May 31.

Marquez, L. (2004). No Distractions? Proposed Title IX Changes Would Allow Separate Classrooms for Girls and Boys. *ABC News*, May 13.

North Carolina School Stops Same-Sex Classes. (2000). *American Civil Liberties Union News*, April 5.

Study: All-girls Schools Don't Improve Test Scores. (1998). *CNN Interactives*, March 12.

Exercise 2 Read the essay above and answer the following questions.

1. Which pattern of opinion essay is used in this essay? Summarize the outline of the essay and figure out why the essay uses this pattern.

   _____

   _____

2. What is the thesis statement of the essay?

   _____

   _____

3. What are the counter-arguments? What are rebuttals? And what are the sources of supporting evidence for each rebuttal?

Counter-arguments	Rebuttals	Sources

Unit 7　History

Writing Practice

Task　The following table is based on the topic "Cellphone, a Blessing or a Curse?". Complete the table by adding some supporting evidence and then write an opinion essay using information from the table.

Cellphone as a blessing		Cellphone as a curse	
Supporting evidence 1		Supporting evidence 1	
Supporting evidence 2		Supporting evidence 2	
Supporting evidence 3		Supporting evidence 3	

UNIT 8

Psychology

Introduction

As one of the research fields of parapsychology, telepathy has always been a controversial topic in the scientific community, and its existence is still arousing fierce debate in the academic community. Since the 1970s, parapsychologists have conducted various scientific experiments on telepathy, trying to find evidence of its existence. As one of the sub-disciplines of psychology, the psychology of innovation has attracted wide attention. Professor Robert B. Cialdini analyzes the psychological characteristics of innovation and explores the reasons for the failure of corporate innovation. What do you think are the research results of these parapsychologists? What should a manager do to create a truly innovative culture? In this unit, you'll read two texts which might help you get some information about the two questions.

Learning Objectives

Reading

- Understanding the studies of telepathy and the psychological characteristics of innovation
- Identifying the essay structure of a psychological study
- Summarizing the main ideas using topic-related words and phrases
- Developing ideas about telepathy and psychology of innovation

Writing

- Understanding the purposes of a process essay
- Identifying the features of a process essay
- Mastering the format of a process essay
- Writing a process essay using proper format

Unit 8 Psychology

Topic Exploration

Step 1 Work in groups to discuss the following questions.
- Do you think people can communicate by thought alone?
- What do you know about telepathy?
- Have you ever had any telepathic experience? If so, share within your group.

Step 2 One student from each group reports the discussion results to the whole class.

Step 3 Watch a video about telepathy. Figure out its main idea and discuss it with your partner.

Reading

Telepathy[1]

Can human beings communicate by thought alone? For more than a century the issue of telepathy[2] has divided the scientific community, and

---

1 This text is adapted from *Cambridge English: IELTS 8*. (2011). Cambridge: Cambridge University Press.

2 telepathy: the ability to communicate without the use of the five senses. It's an instinct which can be woken up in times of emergency or need. When we feel that something is happening or about to happen by instinct, we're using resources within the unconscious mind. When the resources of two persons' unconscious minds link together into the same frequency, we call it telepathy.

even today it still sparks bitter controversy among top academics.

1   Since the 1970s, parapsychologists[3] at leading universities and research institutes around the world have risked the **derision** of skeptical colleagues by putting the various claims for telepathy to the test in dozens of **rigorous** scientific studies. The results and their implications are dividing even the researchers who uncovered them.

2   Some researchers say the results constitute compelling evidence that telepathy is genuine. Other parapsychologists believe the field is **on the brink of** collapse, having tried to produce **definitive** scientific proof and failed. Sceptics and advocates alike do **concur on** one issue, however: that the most impressive evidence so far has come from the so-called "ganzfeld" experiments[4], a German term that means "whole field". Reports of telepathic experiences had by people during meditation led parapsychologists to suspect that telepathy might involve "signals" passing between people that were so faint that they were usually **swamped** by normal brain activity. In this case, such signals might be more easily detected by those experiencing meditation-like tranquility in a relaxing "whole field" of light, sound and warmth.

3   The ganzfeld experiment tries to recreate these conditions with participants sitting in soft **reclining chairs** in a sealed room, listening to relaxing sounds while their eyes are covered with special filters letting in only soft pink light. In early ganzfeld experiments, the telepathy test involved identification of a picture chosen from a random selection of four taken from a large image bank. The idea was that a person acting as a "sender" would attempt to **beam** the image

---

3 parapsychologist: someone who is trained in parapsychology. Parapsychology is a field of study concerned with the investigation of paranormal and psychic phenomena which include telepathy, precognition, clairvoyance, psychokinesis, near-death experiences, reincarnation, apparitional experiences, and other paranormal claims.

4 "ganzfeld" experiment: The word "ganzfeld" means "entire field" in German. It is a technique used in the field of parapsychology to test individuals for extrasensory perception (ESP). It uses homogeneous and unpatterned sensory stimulation to produce an effect similar to sensory deprivation. The deprivation of patterned sensory input is said to be conducive to inwardly generated impressions.

over to the "receiver" relaxing in the sealed room. Once the session was over, this person was asked to identify which of the four images had been used. Random guessing would give a hit-rate of 25 per cent; if telepathy is real, however, the hit-rate would be higher. In 1982, the results from the first ganzfeld studies were analyzed by one of its pioneers, the American parapsychologist Charles Honorton. They pointed to typical hit-rates of better than 30 per cent—a small effect, but one which statistical tests suggested could not be **put down to** chance.

4   The implication was that the ganzfeld method had revealed real evidence for telepathy. But there was a crucial flaw in this argument—one routinely overlooked in more conventional areas of science. Just because chance had been ruled out as an explanation did not prove telepathy must exist; there were many other ways of getting positive results. These ranged from "sensory **leakage**"—where clues about the pictures accidentally reach the receiver—to **outright** fraud. In response, the researchers issued a review of all the ganzfeld studies done up to 1985 to show that 80 per cent had found statistically significant evidence. However, they also agreed that there were still too many problems in the experiments which could lead to positive results, and they drew up a list demanding new standards for future research.

5   After this, many researchers switched to autoganzfeld tests—an automated variant of the technique which used computers to perform many of the key tasks such as the random selection of images. By minimizing human involvement, the idea was to minimize the risk of flawed results. In 1987, results from hundreds of autoganzfeld tests were studied by Honorton in a **"meta-analysis"**, statistical technique for finding the overall results from a set of studies. Though less compelling than before, the outcome was still impressive.

6   Yet some parapsychologists remain disturbed by the lack of consistency between individual ganzfeld studies. Defenders of telepathy point out that demanding impressive evidence from every study ignores one basic statistical fact: it takes large samples to

detect small effects. If, as current results suggest, telepathy produces hit-rates only **marginally** above the 25 per cent expected by chance, it's unlikely to be detected by a typical ganzfeld study involving around 40 people: the group is just not big enough. Only when many studies are combined in a meta-analysis will the faint signal of telepathy really become apparent. And that is what researchers do seem to be finding.

7   What they are certainly not finding, however, is any change in attitude of mainstream scientists: most still totally reject the very idea of telepathy. The problem stems at least in part from the lack of any **plausible** mechanism for telepathy.

8   Various theories have been put forward, many focusing on **esoteric** ideas from theoretical physics. They include "**quantum entanglement**"[5], in which events affecting one group of atoms instantly affect another group, no matter how far apart they may be. While physicists have demonstrated entanglement with specially prepared atoms, no one knows if it also exists between atoms making up human minds. Answering such questions would transform parapsychology. This has **prompted** some researchers to argue that the future lies not in collecting more evidence for telepathy, but in probing possible mechanisms. Some work has begun already, with researchers trying to identify people who are particularly successful in autoganzfeld trials. Early results show that creative and artistic people do much better than average: in one study at the University of Edinburgh, musicians achieved a hit-rate of 56 per cent. Perhaps more tests like these will eventually give the researchers the evidence they are seeking and strengthen the case for the existence of telepathy.

---

5   quantum entanglement: a physical resource, like energy, associated with the peculiar nonclassical correlations that are possible between separated quantum systems. Entanglement can be measured, transformed, and purified.

Words and Phrases

beam /biːm/   *v.* to send a radio or television signal through the air, especially to somewhere very distant 发射电波；播送
- *e.g.* Live pictures of the ceremony were beamed around the world.

concur on   to agree with someone on something 就……意见一致，同意
- *e.g.* The brothers rarely concur on any issues.

definitive /dɪˈfɪnətɪv/   *adj.* final; not able to be changed 最终的，决定性的；最佳的
- *e.g.* None can provide a definitive answer to the question of whom resources should be spent on.

derision /dɪˈrɪʒən/   *n.* a strong feeling that somebody or something is silly and not worth considering seriously, shown by laughing in an unkind way or by making unkind remarks 嘲笑；取笑
- *e.g.* His speech was greeted with derision by opposition leaders.

entanglement /ɪnˈtæŋɡəlmənt/   *n.* a difficult situation or relationship that is hard to escape from 纠缠；纠葛；牵连
- *e.g.* The book describes the complex emotional entanglements between the members of the group.

esoteric /ˌesəˈterɪk/   *adj.* known and understood by only a few people who have special knowledge about something 深奥的，只有内行才懂的
- *e.g.* How we regulate insurance is not an esoteric issue.

leakage /ˈliːkɪdʒ/   *n.* the deliberate spreading of secret information 泄漏；透露
- *e.g.* After the leakage of the report, everyone was ringing up about it.

marginally /ˈmɑːdʒənəli/   *adv.* not enough to make an important difference 稍微，略微
- *e.g.* They now cost marginally more than they did last year.

meta-analysis /ˌmetə əˈnæləsɪs/   *n.* a quantitative statistical analysis of several separate but similar experiments or studies in order to test the pooled data for statistical

			significance 元分析；综合分析
		e.g.	This meta-analysis provides a useful overview, including raising issues with the current evidence.
on the brink of			to be very close to being in an unpleasant or dangerous situation 濒于；濒临
		e.g.	The Russian peasantry stood on the brink of disappearance.
outright	/ˈaʊtraɪt/	adj.	complete and total 完全的；彻底的；绝对的
		e.g.	No one party is expected to gain an outright majority.
plausible	/ˈplɔːzəbəl/	adj.	reasonable and likely to be true or successful 似乎是真的；貌似有理的
		e.g.	His story certainly sounds plausible.
prompt	/prɒmpt/	v.	to make people say or do something as a reaction 促使；导致；激起
		e.g.	His speech prompted an angry outburst from a man in the crowd.
put... down to			to think that something is caused by something else 归咎于，归因于
		e.g.	I was having difficulty reading, which I put down to the poor light.
quantum	/ˈkwɒntəm/	n.	a unit of energy in nuclear physics 量子
		e.g.	In the quantum theory of gravity, on the other hand, a third possibility arises.
reclining chair			an armchair whose back can be lowered and foot can be raised to allow the sitter to recline in it 躺椅；活动靠背扶手椅
		e.g.	He leaned back in his reclining chair, gripping its arms firmly, and wondered what was happening to him.
rigorous	/ˈrɪɡərəs/	adj.	careful, thorough, and exact 严密的，缜密的；严谨的
		e.g.	The work failed to meet their rigorous standards.
swamp	/swɒmp/	v.	to suddenly give someone a lot of work, problems, etc. to deal with 使不堪承受；使应接不暇
		e.g.	We've been swamped with phone calls since the advert appeared.

Unit 8 Psychology

Reading Comprehension

Task 1 Text A can be divided into the following five sections. Read the text carefully and work in pairs to find the main idea of each section. Then complete the following table.

Section	Main Idea
Introduction (Paras. 1–2)	• Parapsychologists with differing attitudes towards telepathy. Some say the results constitute compelling evidence that _____; others believe _____ _____. However, they do agree on one issue that _____.
Ganzfeld studies (Paras. 3–4)	• The tests involved a person acting as a _____, who picked out one _____ from a random selection of four, and a _____, who then tried to _____ it. • Results analyzed from the first ganzfeld studies showed the hit-rates were _____ than with random selection, though of a small effect, yet could not be put down to _____. • But there was a crucial claw in the argument: there were many other ways of getting positive results, ranging from _____ to _____.
Autoganzfeld studies (Paras. 5–6)	• To minimize _____, _____ were used for many of the key tasks to reduce _____ _____ in carrying out the tests. • The test results were studied in _____. Though less compelling than before, the outcome was _____ _____. • Yet some parapsychologists remained disturbed by _____ between different tests results which was put down to the basic fact that _____.
Attitude of the mainstream scientists (Para. 7)	• Most of them still _____ partly because of _____.
Conclusion (Para. 8)	• The future of parapsychology lies not in _____ _____, but in _____.

Task 2 Based on the information in the table in Task 1, write a summary of the text in 80–100 words. Try to make your paragraph logical and coherent.

Task 3 Work in groups to discuss the following questions.

1. What are the different opinions of parapsychologists on telepathy?
2. How do the autoganzfeld tests improve the previous ganzfeld studies?
3. Under what conditions might the faint signals of telepathy become really apparent?
4. What will be the future development trend of telepathy studies?
5. Do you believe in the existence of telepathy? And why?

Vocabulary

Task 1 For each sentence there are four choices marked A, B, C, and D. Choose the one that best keeps the meaning with the underlined part.

1. Try processing all the relevant information contained in the problem to help you come up with one plausible explanation.

    A. reasonable   B. incredible   C. improbable   D. inconceivable

2. The governor's plan was greeted with derision by most journalists and pundits.

    A. advocacy   B. respect   C. ridicule   D. applause

3. Factual and forensic evidence makes a suicide verdict the most compelling answer to the mystery of his death.

    A. flimsy   B. fascinating   C. hollow   D. credible

4. Pictures of the famine were beamed to television audiences all over the world.

    A. transformed   B. transmitted   C. transcoded   D. transacted

5. I was skeptical when the doctor suggested I try massage for my headaches, but it really helped.

    A. agnostic   B. convinced   C. confident   D. dubious

Unit 8 Psychology

6. To my untutored eye that just looks like a load of random brush strokes and yet it's a very valuable painting.

   A. haphazard B. deliberate C. systematic D. structured

7. Perhaps there is less to fight about, with the country in a period of tranquility and the dangers of drug abuse and other unwholesome behavior well known.

   A. peace B. commotion C. business D. confusion

8. Other parapsychologists believe the field is on the brink of collapse, having tried to produce definitive scientific proof and failed.

   A. arbitrary B. absolute C. authoritative D. inclusive

9. A fatal flaw in your argument is your trust that the other side will keep the agreement.

   A. gap B. credit C. merit D. mistake

10. He says that an investment trust is particularly suited to an esoteric investment idea such as Chinese sustainable growth.

    A. simple B. complicated C. familiar D. significant

Task 2 Complete the following sentences with the words and phrases given below. Change the form if necessary.

rigorous	faint	outright	leakage
marginal	prompt	concur on	on the brink of
put... down to	rule out		

1. She sets up a(n) _____ intellectual framework to deconstruct various categories of film.

2. Recent worries over the president's health have _____ speculation over his political future.

3. The company had huge debts and was _____ collapse.

4. Sometimes _____ of secret information come out in newspaper stories accidentally.

161

5. These cameras have increased only _____ in value over the past decade.

6. A group of automotive engineers testing the horsepower of an engine would be expected to _____ how powerful the engine is.

7. Women are twice as likely as men to get skin cancer. Experts _____ this _____ the fact that they're more fond of sunbathing.

8. The police have _____ homicide, saying Hall either fell from the high waterfront walkway or committed suicide.

9. The response of the audience varied from _____ rejection to warm hospitality.

10. There is now only a(n) _____ hope that any of the crewmen have survived the sinking of the freighter.

Translation

Task 1 *Translate the following paragraph into Chinese.*

Reports of telepathic experiences had by people during meditation led parapsychologists to suspect that telepathy might involve "signals" passing between people that were so faint that they were usually swamped by normal brain activity. In this case, such signals might be more easily detected by those experiencing meditation-like tranquility in a relaxing "whole field" of light, sound and warmth.

Task 2 Translate the following paragraph into English with the help of the words in brackets.

多数外教认为中国学生在课堂上不善言谈，有人解释说这是因为学生担心回答错误而成为同伴的嘲笑对象。这似乎是一个合乎情理的解释，但我却不认同。这里有着更深刻的文化因素，比如，中国教师往往批评多而鼓励少，尤其是对爱说话的孩子，这就使学生在课堂上更倾向于保持沉默。(put... down to, derision, plausible, concur on, prompt)

The Psychology of Innovation
Read **Text B** online and do the exercises.

Process Essay

Introduction

Process essay is a common type of essay in academic study. One of its purposes is to give readers instructions by describing steps of how to do something clearly. For example, "How to write an academic essay?" and "How to conduct academic research?" are topics related to giving instructions. Another purpose is to give readers information about how something happens. "How do nuclear power plants work?" and "How does the infant learn to speak?" are topics showing this purpose.

Exercise 1 Have you written a process essay before? What's the topic? And what's your writing purpose?

_____

_____

Features of a Process Essay

Below are the features of a process essay.

Patterns of organization	The supporting paragraphs in most process essays are arranged in chronological order (time order).
Supporting details	All the supporting details should be described clearly and vividly, and organized in a logical order. Background information should be provided if readers are unfamiliar with the topic.

Transitional signals	In the process essay, time signals are usually frequently used to indicate the time order of the process, such as *first, second, then, finally, at first, later, next, at last, after, before, meanwhile, as, soon, now, during*, etc.

Format of a Process Essay

The format of a process essay contains three parts: introduction, main body and conclusion.

Introduction		Background information Thesis statement
Main body	Step 1	Topic sentence 1 Supporting details
	Step 2	Topic sentence 2 Supporting details
	Step 3	Topic sentence 3 Supporting details
Conclusion		Summary/Prediction/Recommendation

In the introduction, the background information about the topic is provided, such as *when*, *why*, and *in what situation* the procedure is used. Normally the last sentence is the thesis statement in which the importance of the process is explained or the writer's opinion on the process is expressed, and the main steps might be included as well. The main body contains three main steps, although there might be more detailed steps. You need to divide them into three main steps and write a topic sentence for each step. In addition, the three steps are usually arranged in time order. Finally, there are some methods to conclude the essay, such as summary (to summarize the essay by restating the main steps), prediction (to describe the results of the procedure), and recommendation (to give advice or suggestions about the procedure or the topic).

Exercise 2 Read the text below and finish the tasks.

Staying Positive in the Workplace

It is understandable that workers are discontented in the workplace. Especially in these days, there is often a general atmosphere of anxiety and despondency at work because of insecurity: the economy is depressed and many companies are downsizing, restructuring and making redundancies. It is, however, necessary that they should strive to be more positive. On average, people spend about a third of their lives at work. That's a lot of time to be miserable or depressed. Therefore, it's important to learn how to stay positive in the workplace.

Firstly, take good care of yourself. To begin with, pay attention to your physical health: eating a wholesome diet, doing exercise and having sufficient sleep. If work has taken over your life, find a balance: find and nurture friendships outside of work and do something in your free time that is totally unrelated to your job. Remember also to take care of your appearance and dress well to boost your self-esteem in the workplace.

Secondly, stay in a good mood in the workplace. Avoid negative co-workers if possible; if not, try to put a more positive spin on what they say, tell a joke, or just remain neutral. Focus on the good things rather than the bad, and smile more often—your affirmative attitude may rub off on your colleagues. If it is possible, listen to light, uplifting music if you feel it helps—as long as it does not distract you from your work.

Finally, empower yourself with knowledge. If job security is causing anxiety, developing professional competence is essential. Expand your skill set—take a course, become familiar with a new computer program, tackle new tasks—and consider shouldering more responsibility if you are not already overworked. Perhaps it is time to set new goals, even minor ones. Being pro-active and creative will not only keep you focused, motivated and more in control of your work life but also prepare you for the job market if the worst should happen.

Staying positive despite this is a challenge but it is important not to develop a negative attitude at work, especially if you already have a stressful workload. Beware: chronic negativity may lead to long-term psychological and physical ill health. On the other hand, optimists have a greater sense of self-worth and are thus more likely to experience job satisfaction through an appreciation of their own achievements and productivity. If workplace tension is getting you down, it is time to take stock of the situation and establish a more positive outlook.

1. The above is a typical process essay. Read the essay and complete the table with key information from the text.

Introduction	Thesis statement: _____
Step 1	Topic sentence: _____
Step 2	Topic sentence: _____
Step 3	Topic sentence: _____
Conclusion	Which method is used in the concluding paragraph? _____ A. Summary. B. Prediction. C. Recommendation.

2. Figure out the detailed information of the essay.

1) Rewrite the thesis statement to make it more specific.

2) How many examples are given to support the topic sentence in the second paragraph? Do you think the examples are vivid and clear enough?

3) If you were the author, what examples would you provide to support the topic sentence in the second paragraph? Rewrite the first supporting paragraph.

4) Find out the transitional signals in the three topic sentences.

Sample Essay Analysis

Young Children's Sense of Identity

A sense of self develops in young children by degrees. The process can usefully be thought of in terms of the gradual emergence of two somewhat separate features: the self as a subject, and the self as an object. William James introduced the distinction in 1892, and contemporaries of his, such as Charles Cooley, added to the developing debate. Ever since then psychologists have continued building on the theory.

According to James, a child's first step on the road to self-understanding can be seen as the recognition that he or she exists. This is an aspect of the self that he labelled "self-as-subject", and he gave it various elements. These included an awareness of one's own agency (i.e. one's power to act), and an awareness of one's distinctiveness from other people. These features gradually emerge as infants explore their world and interact with caregivers. Cooley (1902) suggested that a sense of the self-as-subject was primarily concerned with being able to exercise power. He proposed that the earliest examples of this are an infant's attempts to control physical objects, such as toys or his or her own limbs. This is followed by attempts to affect the behavior of other people. For example, infants learn that when they cry or smile someone responds to them.

Another powerful source of information for infants about the effects they can have on the world around them is provided when others mimic them. Many parents spend a lot of time, particularly in the early months, copying their infant's vocalizations and expressions. In addition, young children enjoy looking in mirrors, where the movements they can see are dependent upon their own movements. This is not to say that infants recognize the reflection as their own image (a later development). However, Lewis and Brooks-Gunn (1979) suggest that infants' developing understanding that the movements they see in the mirror are contingent on their own, leads to a growing awareness that they are distinct from other people. This is because they, and only they, can change the reflection in the mirror.

This understanding that children gain of themselves as active agents continues to develop in their attempts to co-operate with others in play. Dunn (1988) points out that it is in such day-to-day relationships and interactions that the child's understanding of himself or herself emerges. Empirical investigations of the "self-as-subject" in young children are, however, rather scarce because of difficulties of communication: even if young infants can reflect on their experience, they certainly cannot express this aspect of the self directly.

Once children have acquired a certain level of self-awareness, they begin to place themselves in a whole series of categories, which together play such an important part in defining them uniquely as "themselves". This second step in the development of a full sense of self is what James called the "self-as-object". This has been seen by many to be the aspect of the self which is most influenced by social elements, since it is made up of social roles (such as student, brother, colleague) and characteristics which derive their meaning from comparison or interaction with other people (such as trustworthiness, shyness, sporting ability).

Cooley and other researchers suggested a close connection between a person's own understanding of their identity and other people's understanding of it. Cooley believed that people build up their sense of identity from the reactions of others to them, and from the view they believe others have of them. He called the self- as-object the "looking-glass self", since people come to see themselves as they are reflected in others. Mead (1934) went even further, and saw the self and the social world as inextricably bound together: "The self is essentially a social structure, and it arises in social experience... it is impossible to conceive of a self arising outside of social experience."

Lewis and Brooks-Gunn argued that an important developmental milestone is reached when children become able to recognize themselves visually without the support of seeing contingent movement. This recognition occurs around their second birthday. In one experiment, Lewis and Brooks-Gunn (1979) dabbed some red powder on the noses of children who were playing in front of a mirror, and then observed how often they touched their noses. The psychologists reasoned that if the children knew what they usually looked like, they would be surprised by the unusual red mark and would start touching it. On the other hand, they found that children of 15 to 18 months are generally not able to recognize themselves unless other cues such as movement are present.

Finally, perhaps the most graphic expressions of self-awareness in general can be seen in the displays of rage which are most common from 18 months to 3 years of age. In a longitudinal study of groups of three or four children, Bronson (1975) found that the intensity of the frustration and anger in their disagreements increased sharply between the ages of 1 and 2 years. Often, the children's disagreements involved a struggle over a toy that none of them had played with before or after the tug-of-war: the children seemed to be disputing ownership rather than wanting to play with it. Although it may be less marked in other societies, the link between the sense of "self" and of "ownership" is a notable feature of childhood in Western societies.

Exercise 3   Read the essay above and answer the following questions.

1. This essay doesn't follow the traditional format of a process essay. Complete the outline and find out how it is different from the traditional process essay.

Introduction (Para(s). _____)	Thesis statement: _____
Main body (Para(s). _____)	Step 1 (Para(s). _____) Topic sentence: _____ Step 2 (Para(s). _____) Topic sentence: _____

2. Do you now have a clear picture of the development of the young children's sense of identity? Describe it and give reasons to support your opinion.

   _____
   _____

3. How many examples does the author use to support the point that a sense of the "self-as-subject" was primarily concerned with being able to exercise power?

   _____
   _____

4. Complete the following chart about the process of children's development of "self-as-object".

Age	Sense of identity during this period
15 to 18 months	
2 years old	
1 to 2 years old	
18 months to 3 years old	

Unit 8 Psychology

Writing Practice

Task Below is an article about how to set up a safe home work base for telecommuting, but it doesn't follow the traditional process essay format as the main body doesn't fall into three parts with a topic sentence at the beginning. Read the text carefully and rewrite it based on the format you have learned in this unit.

Setting up a Safe Home Work Base for Telecommuting

Working from home can be a flexible and money-saving option for modern businesses, but a company may be legally liable for any injury sustained by the home-based employee.

Before arranging to work from home, telecommuters must identify any potential health and safety issues by following these steps.

Identify hazards that could harm those who visit, live or work in your home. Imagine your home as an office environment and examine possible lighting, ventilation, tripping or electrical hazards.

Minimize the risk-falls are the most common household accident but are easily prevented. Start with the floor: shift chairs, desks or cabinets that impede progress from one area to another, and make sure that, as far as possible, all work desks and other items are arranged round the edges of the space.

Get rid of loose floor coverings such as small carpets, or use only those with a non-slip backing. If possible, use non-slip mats under office chairs to avoid the possibility of unwanted movement. Pick up any objects that are on the floor (books, shoes, boxes, etc.).

Carefully examine your workplace environment, and ensure that lamp, telephone or extension cords and computer leads are off the floor to avoid the chance of tripping and falling. Taping these along the edge of the wall above the skirting board and over doorways is one option, or alternatively, you may need to employ an electrician to install more outlets.

Next, look at the stairs and steps both inside and outside your home. Keep steps and stairs clear; fix any steps that are loose or not level; if carpeted, ensure the carpet is firmly attached, or attach non-slip rubber treads to uncarpeted steps; where there are loose or absent handrails, install new ones; ensure stairs and steps are well lit (change to more powerful wall lighting than normal).

Create a comprehensive inventory of necessary repair work and/or new installations and follow through on your risk controls.

Hold a forum with your household members to promote safety consciousness and hazard awareness and run through safety drills; get household members compliance on issues of tidiness, cleanliness, etc.

Both parties must remember that health and safety obligations apply the same way to work performed in a home-based workplace as they do in the office. After the risk assessment and fixes have been completed, the workplace manager must inspect the workplace with the employee and both should sign off on the findings of the inspection.

"清华社英语在线"(TUP English Online)平台使用指南

"清华社英语在线"集教、学、练、测、评、研等功能于一体,支持全媒体教学的泛在式外语学习。PC、移动端同步应用,提供互动式的教学环境、个性化的学习管理、多维度的学情监控、碎片化的应用场景,以实现混合式教学。平台基于数据设计,致力于全方位提高教学效率、提升教学效果、优化学习体验,为高校英语教师和学生提供在线学习、交流、教学管理、测试评估等服务。

一、数字课程使用指南

Step 1:登录平台(PC端、移动端均可)

PC端:www.tsinghuaelt.com(推荐使用360或Google Chrome浏览器);

移动端:微信内搜索小程序"清华社英语在线"或扫描下方小程序二维码。

Step 2:输入账号(登录账号、密码由平台创建)

(1)集体用户(学校教师统一授课)

由任课教师联系出版社,平台为学生统一创建登录账号。教师在平台开课后,学生进入教师课程学习;

（2）个人用户

登录界面点击【帮助中心】，联系平台在线客服获取账号密码，随后进入平台的公共课程内学习。

Step 3：激活课程（本书封底贴有教材配套验证码，输入以激活课程）

（1）进入教师课程后，点击【激活教材码】，刮开本书封底贴的激活码序列号并输入，即可激活课程开始学习；

（2）进入公共课程后，同上述方式激活课程后开始学习。

二、特别提示

1. 每本教材配套的激活码仅可在一个登录账号的配套课程中使用，激活成功后即失效，不可重复使用；

2. 激活码在成功激活课程后的使用期限为一年，请在开学初仅输入需要学习的课程的激活码；如因过早输入非本学期所学课程的激活码，导致课程届时过期而无法使用，我社不负责补发激活码；

3. 激活码遗失不补，需联系教师或自行购买新的教材或激活码。

三、帮助中心

数字课程及平台使用的常见问题，请在登录界面或课程内的【帮助中心–常见问题】处点击查看；如有其他疑问，请咨询平台在线客服。